D0436662

Depression

Depression

Finding Hope & Meaning
In Life's Darkest Shadow

DON BAKER
EMERY NESTER

MULTNOMAH PRESS
PORTLAND, OREGON 97266

Scripture quotations are from the New American Standard Bible, copyright The Lockman Foundation 1960, 1961, 1962, 1963, 1968, 1971, 1972, 1973, 1975, 1977. Used by permission.

Some names of the people and places appearing in this book have been changed to maintain the anonymity of persons and events. Similarities of fictionalized characters and circumstances to actual people and events are not intended.

DEPRESSION: Finding Hope and Meaning in Life's Darkest Shadow
© 1983 by Don Baker, Emery Nester
Published by Multnomah Press
Portland, Oregon 97266

Printed in the United States of America

Second Printing 1983

Library of Congress Cataloging in Publication Data

Baker, Donald R.
    Depression: Finding hope and meaning in life's darkest shadow.

    1. Depression, Mental—Patients—United States—Biography.
2. Clergy—United States—Biography. 3. Baker, Donald R.
I. Nester, Emery.   II. Title.
RC537.B334   1983   616.85'27'00924 [B]   82-24609
ISBN 0-88070-011-4

To Martha,
who faithfully
supported her husband
in his time of great need,

and

to Mary Ann,
who willingly
shared her husband
in his time of great challenge.

Contents

Foreword

It's a Sunday evening. It's been a beautiful, cool, sunny day in Fullerton. I'm sitting in my favorite spot in our home—a lovely enclosed patio. It's like an indoor garden with lots of plants and two sofas surrounding our favorite old black Franklin stove. A fire has been burning for hours, earlier shared with some dear friends from Waco.

Watching the flames dance from the burning coals, I find myself reflecting for a moment on my past. It is difficult to believe my life was darkened by depression for so long—*fifteen years*.

Depression . . . black as a thousand midnights in a cypress swamp. Loneliness that is indescribable. Confusion regarding God. Frustration with life and circumstances. The feeling that you have been abandoned, that you are worthless. Unloveable. The pain is excruciating.

The roots of depression lie much deeper than our twentieth century living-in-the-fast-lane lifestyle. The very first recorded incident of depression is in Genesis 4. Cain's offering of the fruit from the ground had not been regarded by God. Upon learning that, Cain became angry and depressed. God told Cain, "If you do right, will there not be a lifting up? But if you misbehave, sin is crouching at the door; its intention is toward you, and you must master it" (Genesis 4:7, Berkeley[1]). God's instructions for getting out of the pit emphasized actions of obedience—regardless of feelings.

Did Cain choose to respond to God and do what was right? No. Instead, he had words with his brother Abel and then killed him. Cain chose not to assume any responsibility for his downcast spirit; he did not master his attitudes.

7

Perhaps those few words hold the key that unlocks the door to the black pit of depression. But knowing the responsible way out is sometimes as elusive as a mirage in the desert.

Chuck and I first met Don Baker at a Mount Hermon family conference in the summer of 1979. We immediately fell in love with him and Martha, his wife, and had a grand time during the conference.

One evening Don chose to speak publicly, for the first time, about his own past in the black pit. His vivid imagery immediately brought painful memories to mind. My thoughts returned to the previous spring when Chuck and I had experienced some deep hurts in our Christian service. For the first time in our twenty-four years of ministry, we were both depressed. At the same time. The pain of that experience lasted for nearly four months. But even more vividly, I was reminded of a now distant past when depression had been my own constant companion. So many of the thoughts Don expressed about his depression were feelings I too had shared.

With much emotion I waited until everyone had cleared from Don's presence after the meeting. Then, with my back to those still in the auditorium, I wept with Don. I commended him for his courage to communicate in such a manner and expressed how I had never possessed such courage. His manner of openness had shown me how effectively our lives can minister—providing examples for others in their walk with God through the inevitable change and pain of life.

One of the most beautiful aspects of walking with a sovereign God is His ability to orchestrate the interchange of lives—at just the right moment—to accomplish His own divine plan. The entry of Emery Nester into Don's world during his struggle certainly verified this truth.

Emery had been in the pastorate, and at the time of his meetings with Don, he was a psychologist. Their paths crossed when both were in the pit—hardly a situation providing much hope. I love Emery's persistent pursuit of Don, and his true example of a godly love. He saw Don weekly and spent 100 hours counseling him. Wouldn't it be great if we all had such a claim to friendship?

Even though I wasn't there, I'm confident their time together was marked by a constant attempt to know what was right so they could "do what was right." I'm sure they measured every thought and action against God's Word, though at times their feelings claimed that those truths were lies.

Indeed, insofar as is humanly possible, they came to master their attitudes and finally experience the lifting of their spirits and countenances. They were free. They *are* free.

This book is the result of their pilgrimage, and how privileged we are to be allowed access to that segment of their lives. I know their exposure comes from an intense desire to assist in lifting others from that dismal pit.

If you find the pit your habitat, let me suggest that you read these pages slowly and embellish their words with your own experiences.

Think constantly "what is my responsibility to the circumstances of this day, to the information I have just received?" Then follow through with actions. God instructs us to obey . . . He doesn't say to wait until we *feel* like obeying.

It is my prayer, along with the prayers of Don and Emery, that you will find these insights helpful for you as well as those you love. *Depression* is truly a book of hope and encouragement.

Cynthia Swindoll
Executive Director, Insight for Living

---

[1]*The Modern Language Bible, The New Berkeley Version in Modern English,* copyright 1945, 1959, 1969 by Zondervan Publishing House.

Preface

It is impossible for those who have never been depressed to fully understand the deep, perplexing pain that depression causes.

For four interminable years I appeared healthy, without bandages and without crutches. There were no visible scars, no bleeding, and yet there was the endless, indefinable pain that no doctor's probing fingers could locate—no drug could totally relieve. There was always the pain and along with it the desire for oblivion—an oblivion that would only come in minute snatches of restless sleep.

I seemed to be out of touch with reality. Life was a blur, often out of focus. My life seemed to be nothing but pretense and fantasy. No one really cared, I felt—not even God. The only solution—at times—seemed to be suicide.

To be told that Christians never get depressed only pushed me deeper into my black hole of depression.

The way out of that black hole was a long and painful process—one that required the sensitive and insightful counsel of a friend.

Emery walked with me in my blackness and gradually, but persistently, helped me to unravel the shroud that had forced darkness upon me.

I narrate Part 1 of this book, and Emery discusses depression in Part 2. As we combine our memories and insights, it is our purpose to help you better understand depression and to see that Christians can and do experience it, family and friends can help you through it, and God can use it to enhance and enrich your life.

Don Baker

PART 1

THE PATH OF EXPERIENCE

Don Baker

"Lord, all my desire is before Thee;
And my sighing is not hidden from Thee.
My heart throbs, my strength fails me;
And the light of my eyes,
even that has gone from me."
Psalm 38:9-10

Chapter 1

Ward 7E

I had visited Ward 7E many times. Its institutional yellow walls and highly polished floors resembled most of the psychiatric wards and mental hospitals where I had gone to minister to members of my congregation.

There's always a certain apprehension that lurks in the shadows of one's mind while walking down those sterile, silent corridors. Behind each door is a different story. I've listened to them all. The criminally insane, the suicidal, the depressed, the alcoholic, the hostile, the addict, and then on many occasions I've tried to talk to those who have forgotten how to respond.

I've never felt comfortable with the mentally ill.

This time, however, my discomfort had been replaced by fear. My apprehension had given way to feelings of impending doom. The very atmosphere was charged with foreboding glimpses of the unpredictable. I was traumatized with humiliation and embarrassment. I was struggling against a creeping hostility waiting to overpower me.

This time I was being led down the silent halls of Ward 7E, not as a pastor but as a patient.

For years I had struggled to understand the unpredictable mood swings that could carry me from peaks of elation to the deep valleys of despair.

I could preach with fervor and power, I could share Christ with enthusiasm and success. I would counsel with meaningful insight and socialize with sheer delight. But without warning, any or all of these positive and delightful emotions would suddenly be forced to give way to feelings of gloom and periods of weakness. I would withdraw, and a form of paranoia would settle in. I would suddenly be overwhelmed with feelings of inadequacy and inferiority. On occasion I toyed with thoughts of self-destruction.

At times I was convinced that my problem was spiritual. I'd pore over the Scriptures, agonize in prayer, go through periods of confession, dig up any and every negative memory that could be found, and cry to God for deliverance.

At other times I was certain that the problem was physical. "I'm working too hard," I'd tell myself, and I'd then proceed to find ways to lighten the load, or even better, escape for days or weeks in an attempt to find relief. I'd had as many diagnoses as I'd had doctors.

The struggle reached its inevitable climax when I found myself too weary to minister, too filled with hostility to love, and too frightened to preach.

One Sunday morning, I collapsed in tears. A dear brother in Christ, one of my deacons, found me convulsed with sobs, unable to rise and unwilling to even try.

In the weeks and months that followed, the bewildering and overpowering bouts with depression finally led me and my family to agree that the only direction left for me was to seek competent psychiatric care.

As I walked through the steel door into Ward 7E, my one thought was that the life I had known was finished. I would never again be able to enjoy the confidence of a congregation who would trust me to shepherd them.

For days I withdrew into a medicated stupor. I resented sharing a room with one patient who was criminally insane and another who walked around like a zombie.

I refused all offers of help. I resisted any intrusions into my silence. I rejected the many opportunities to visit with friends. The only human who could break through the wall was my wife.

The doctors at this point agreed on only one thing: depression—cause or causes unknown. The term was not a new one to me. It was one, however, that I resisted.

I remembered reading Martin Lloyd-Jones's statement regarding depression. "In a sense a depressed person is a contradiction in terms, and he is a very poor recommendation for the Gospel."[1]

Bob George, director of Discipleship Counseling Services in Dallas, Texas, has stated in a Christian periodical, ". . . as children of God, we don't need to be depressed or defeated in life. God has provided us with everything we need for a life of godliness."[2] He went on to say, "When a believer is not experiencing freedom and joy in the Spirit . . . it can only be that he is nearsighted and blind and has forgotten that he has been cleansed from his past sins (2 Peter 1:9). He has forgotten his position in Christ."[3]

Tim LaHaye states in his book that the primary cause of depression is self-pity. Others have flatly stated that depression is a sin.

To be forced to acknowledge that I was depressed was, to say the least, depressing.

I hated the word. It was tantamount to sin. My limited knowledge of its meaning and its universality compounded my gloom with guilt and my frustration with anger.

In an attempt to help me feel the reality of my problem, various members of the hospital staff began gently asking probing questions:

"How do you feel?"

The answer came slowly and with great difficulty. My first response was, "I don't know." Even my feelings had become elusive and indefinable. When I did "feel" something, the words to describe that feeling came with great difficulty. It seemed that my brain had either stopped functioning or at least had slowed to an almost imperceptible pace.

Slowly the words came. Words like,
"Sad"
    "Empty"
        "Alone"
            "Hopeless"
                "Afraid"
                    "Worthless"
                        "Ambivalent"
                            "Rejected"

"Do you sleep well?"

If I'd had the inner energy, I would have laughed. I finally said, "All the time" and "Never." Sleep was no longer the necessary nightly reviving experience—it was nothing more than an escape-mechanism. I would drift off into a fitful slumber when there was work to be done and remain wide-awake during the interminably long hours of the night.

"How do you feel about your job?"

I'm a failure! I had lost touch with reality completely. My pastoral ministry had always been effective. Thousands had come to Christ. My people loved me. My churches had always grown. I have loved the Scriptures and have been in demand as a Bible teacher. My depression (and I was beginning to use the word more frequently) had completely colored, or rather discolored, my perspective on a fruitful and happy ministry.

"Do you eat well?"

"All the time," I answered. One psychiatrist asked me, "If you had three wishes, what would they be?" I could only think of one. "I'd like to get my weight down to a normal 165 pounds." I didn't know at the time whether depression was the cause of my insatiable cravings or whether my bad eating habits were causing my depression. Others, I understand now, react just the opposite. They lose interest in food. Oh, how I wished I could.

"How do you feel about yourself?"

Inadequate! My self-confidence had hit bottom. There was a total loss of self-esteem.

"How do you feel about your family?"

Unworthy! I know they love me, but I don't deserve their love. I was convinced that the many tender expressions of love from Martha, John, and Kathy were all pretense. They couldn't love me—not in the condition I was in.

"How often do you and your wife have sex?"

I couldn't remember. Not only had my interest in sex lessened, but at times I had even feared impotence.

"Are you having difficulty making decisions?"

I could hardly decide how to answer the question. For weeks I struggled with whether or not to resign my pastorate. I would read one verse of Scripture that seemed to tell me to stay and another that suggested just the opposite. I would get different answers each time I prayed.

I never was able to make that decision by myself.

"Do you like to be around people?"

"No!" An emphatic "no." "Please," I said, "just leave me alone."

"Are you often angry?"

With this question I buried my head and began to sob. "Oh yes, and always with the ones I love the most." My wife had felt the sting of unpredicted and uncontrolled anger. My children had begun to cower when I walked by. My deacons, my friends, all of them felt the force of my anger and always without provocation.

"How do you feel when you get angry?"

Guilty! Unforgivably guilty. No one could lift the pall of gloom that settled over me as guilt set in. A thousand *I'm sorry's* made no difference. The changeless promises of God had no effect. I would even feel guilt when there was no cause for it.

"Have you ever thought of suicide?"

Yes. At least once a day. I'm sure that only the grace of God and the graphic memories of seeing so many suicides and struggling with so many shattered lives in the wake of suicide kept me from actually killing myself.

It was a wise and insightful counselor who probed me with those questions and then gently said, "I'm sure, Mr. Baker, that the doctor's original diagnosis is correct. You are deeply depressed—you do need help—you do need to be here—but you'll get better. It will take time, but you'll get better."

Chapter 1, Notes

[1] D. Martin Lloyd-Jones, *Spiritual Depression: Its Causes & Cure* (Grand Rapids: Wm. B. Eerdmans Publishing Co., 1965), p. 11.

[2] Bob George, "There's No Need to Be Depressed," *Moody Monthly*, February 1982, p. 7.

[3] Ibid., p. 10.

". . . my flesh also will abide in hope."
Acts 2:26

Chapter 2

"You'll Get Better"

"You'll get better. It will take time, but you'll get better."
I'll always be grateful for those gentle words—profound in their simplicity—yet filled with hope. And oh, how I needed hope.

For one brief moment there was a slight glimmer of light in my black hole of depression. Not much light—not enough to discern direction, nor to illuminate the many unanswered questions. Not even enough to plot a future, but there was light. It was just enough to enable me to make out the word—Hope.

I fondled and nurtured that word. I cradled it in every waking moment. It was the only word that sustained me through the interminable nights punctuated with endless interruptions and the oftentimes meaningless days filled with frantic activity.

Prior to that bold but simple prophetic pronouncement I had been left dangling between two contrasting points of view.

One group of doctors was convinced that there was nothing wrong with me. Another group had agreed that my problems were so acute and complex that my days of ministry were finished.

Both opinions had devastated me.

But now there was hope, and it was all wrapped up in one brief but authoritative pronouncement: "You'll get better."

Martha's first visit was extremely difficult for both of us.

Upon my arrival at Ward 7E, I had been searched, bathed, and my clothes had been confiscated. When I objected, they simply stated, "Just routine—you'll get them back when you prove you can be trusted with them."

I was dressed in ill-fitting pajamas, a robe that dragged the floor, and slippers two sizes too large.

I was shaved, my teeth were brushed, but I had lost my comb. I must have looked terribly disheveled. It showed on my wife's face for just one brief moment as she was ushered through that heavy steel door. Her cheerful smile gave way momentarily to a look of stunned surprise. She recovered quickly, but was betrayed by two tears that lingered in her beautiful brown eyes.

Those tears were like mirrors in which I saw revealed the Don Baker I had never seen before. I saw myself stripped of all pride, all accomplishments, and all glory. I saw myself as a derelict who had reached bottom. I felt terribly unworthy of this woman I loved so much.

And yet, as I held her in my arms, I could only think of one thing to say. "I'll get better—it may take time, but I'll get better."

John spent the first Sunday afternoon with me. We played a little pool and watched some television. Just before he left I looked up into my growing son's bewildered face and said, "Don't worry, Son, I'll get better—it may take time, but I'll get better."

Kathy brought me a poem, and, in her own shy but beautiful way, told me how much she loved and admired me. As she was ready to leave, I held my eighth grader in my arms and said it again, "Don't worry, Honey, I'll get better. It may take a little time, but I'll get better."

Even Joey came to see me, and as he searched my face with the inquisitive eyes of a shaggy little poodle, I took his head between my hands and said, "Don't worry, Joey; I'll get better. It may take a little time, but I'll get better."

Over and over again during those uncertain and confusing days, I thanked my Lord for a wise and thoughtful counselor who had taken time to give me hope.

Dr. Leonard Crammer writes about the types of depression in his book, *Up From Depression*.

"Depressions vary in intensity and in duration. Depressions may be mild, moderate, or severe. The general rule is that mild depressions, while distressing, can be overcome rather quickly. Moderate and severe depressions are almost always classified as serious and should be managed with medical help.

"The duration of a depression may be *acute, recurrent*, or *chronic*. An *acute depression*, no matter what the reason, comes on quickly and may endure only a week, or as long as four months. It can clear up spontaneously without treatment. A *recurrent depression* is an acute episode that reappears at different intervals with normal periods (called remissions) in between. A *chronic depression* arises more gradually and lingers for an indefinite time, even up to two or more years, with ultimate remission."[1]

My bouts with depression seemed to have been graduating from the mild to the moderate and now to the severe.

For nearly four years I had been experiencing depression in all forms. For four years I had been clinging to the slippery sides of that deep, black hole; sometimes falling, then recovering; then falling and again recovering until finally I could hold on no longer. I had plummeted into the deepest recesses of that impenetrable darkness.

But even as the darkness lingered and deepened, there was now one faint glimmer of light flipped on by a wise and gentle counselor whose name has long since been forgotten.

"You'll get better—it may take time, but you'll get better."

Chapter 2, Notes

[1]Leonard Cammer, *Up From Depression* (New York: Simon & Schuster, 1969), p. 25.

"Jesus wept."
John 11:35

Chapter 3

A Distant Grief

*F*or four years I had searched for the cause of my depression. I viewed every experience of loss with great suspicion.

Any loss, whether it be the loss of health, the loss of a job, the loss of a loved one, the loss of self-esteem, or the loss of reputation, can cause one to become depressed.

Job's case is always among the first that comes to mind whenever we consider loss. His loss began with his possessions, swept over his household to claim his family, and finally resulted in the total loss of his health.

When we find him in Job, chapter 2, he is sitting in a pile of ashes, smitten from head to foot with boils, scraping his body with a scrap of pottery.

- He curses the day he was born (3:1)
- He proceeds to describe life as
     "darkness" and "gloom"
                     and
     "blackness" and "terror" (3:5)
- He calls it a night without dawn (3:9)
- He wishes he had died at birth (3:11)
- He longs for a death that does not come (3:21)
- He describes his unrelenting agony by stating, "the arrows

of the Almighty are within me; their poison my spirit drinks;
the terrors of God are arrayed against me" (6:4).
Job had fallen into his black hole.

Martha and I had had numerous "loss" experiences.

We had lost our first son three months after his birth.

As I carefully examined that loss, along with others we held
dear, a pattern began to emerge.

In three of the four deaths that occurred early in our marriage,
I had deprived myself of the very necessary therapeutic experience
of grief.

I conducted the funerals, prayed with the family, and displayed myself as the strong one.

My father, a deacon in the church, died one month after I
began my first pastoral ministry in the church of which he was a
member. His death occurred at 2:00 A.M. on Saturday. Less than
thirty-four hours later, I was preaching from the pulpit and con-
ducting my first communion service.

In assuming the role of pastor I was depriving myself of the
greater role of son. I refused to display grief. I rejected my humanness. I buried my grief under a pile of foolish assumptions and
suggested to myself that it would be a discredit to my God if I cried.

Twenty-one years later, long after my deep depression set in,
I sat watching a rerun of "Rifleman" on television. It was mid-
night, and I was alone in my little retreat overlooking the Pacific
Ocean.

I don't remember the story line except that during the show
Chuck Connors had a very moving emotional experience as he was
reunited with his long-lost father.

I began to cry. I cried convulsively, continuously, uncon-
trollably. After nearly an hour, I called Martha long distance in
order to hear her voice and to have her pray with me.

At that time the tears were a mystery to us both—just a part of
the depression, we thought.

The next evening I recounted the experience to a friend. He
asked me to tell him about my father.

As I began to talk, I also began to sob. I began to see that I had been carrying an unfinished transaction of grief that had moved to the subconscious and there had bowed down my soul without my mind even being aware of it.

I conducted my grandmother's funeral. I preached at the funeral for my father-in-law. I have been expected to conduct all the funerals for all of my dear friends. At times I have struggled with this deeply, but silently.

My dear friend, M. L. Custis, a doctor with whom I had shared twenty years of growing experiences, became suddenly and unexpectedly ill of a brain tumor. Within twenty-six days of the first diagnosis he was dead.

M. L. had been a constant source of encouragement to me. He had trusted in me when others could only shake their heads in bewilderment. He had loved me, prayed with me, laughed with me, cried with me.

He gave me my first set of golf clubs and then met me on the course in a vain attempt to occasionally break the spell of my work.

On more than one occasion when I was hospitalized in California, he called long distance from Portland. Our conversations were totally unintelligible. There were no words, only sobs.

At the time of his brief but terminal illness I had been laid aside—exhausted and depressed—again forced to temporarily relinquish my duties.

I was unable to be either his pastor or his friend. His brother, Dwight, conducted his funeral. The service, one of the largest and most precious our church had ever experienced, went on without me.

No amount of explaining has ever completely satisfied my absence to the many who loved him so much. I've never been able to satisfactorily explain it to myself.

Being unable to walk in his death with him and with his dear family again deprived me of the privilege of working through my grief. That bothers me to this day.

Weakness? Quite possibly. There are many, I'm sure, who might feel that I'm not drawing from God's grace or that I'm not displaying pastoral strength. But I have decided it's so much better for me to work through my grief while it's still fresh than to allow it to sift down through the cracks to a subconscious world from which it is so difficult and painful to dredge up later.

"Iron sharpens iron,
So one man sharpens another."
Proverbs 27:17

Chapter 4

A Walk with a Friend

I had lost touch completely with reality.
> God was not real
>> Life was not real
>>> Love was not real
>>>> My wife was not real
>>>>> My children were not real
>>>>>> Friends were not real
>>>>>>> I was not real

All of life was pretense and fantasy—I thought.
Life was a blur, completely out of focus.

I wrote out my feelings on separate occasions. Once when I was somewhat lucid and again when I was completely submerged in depression. The statements, perceptions, and value judgments came from the same mind, written by the same hand, in the same notebook. The similarity stops there, however. It seems as I read them that they came from totally different persons on different planets, describing different civilizations.

In my black hole I could see nothing with clarity.

I was suspicious of every statement, rejected every advance, and distrusted every motive.

Martha would say, "I love you," and I could not believe her.

33

Father's Day greetings, birthday cards, and even Christmas presents were mere tokens of traditional human responses that carried neither warmth nor meaning.

I walked down the familiar streets of the quiet suburban neighborhood in which I lived. I saw nothing and heard nothing but the inner cries of a depressed spirit.

Each morning as I looked out at the beautiful shaded yard with its orange blossoms, flowering almond trees, and lush green grass, I saw only gray and felt only gloom.

Climbing out of bed was the most difficult task of each new day.

Martha would draw my attention to the birds. "Hear the mourning doves?" she would ask. I heard nothing. It was as if someone had altered my eardrums so that only life's discordant sounds would penetrate.

At other times, sounds were devastating. The invading noises were loud and penetrating. Even in conversation I would put my fingers to my ears and plead for silence. Two sounds—such as music and conversation—descending on me at the same time would cause pain and disorientation.

Martha loves beautiful things. I've often called her "my eyes." So often when we travel I'm engrossed in mental preparation for scheduled messages, but even the beauty she would describe was unrecognizable.

During one of my many trips to the hospital the darkness lifted momentarily. I was sitting in the privacy of my room, looking out of my fourth floor window—seeing nothing.

For a few exciting moments I became aware of a tree—a perfectly formed California hemlock. I studied its magnificent broad boughs, reaching out in all directions to shade a beautifully manicured lawn.

I saw it towering above me like a pyramid, with its stately green tip silhouetted against the bright blue of the sky. I studied the limb ends with their two-ranked needles, green on the top and silver on the bottom, and the pendulous cones like Christmas tree ornaments that often brushed lightly against my window.

The cinnamon-red bark was intriguing. I wanted to reach out

and peel it off, then touch it and smell it.

It was beautiful—it was not just beautiful, it was magnificent!

I wrote a poem—the first that I could ever remember.

> "Today I saw a tree.
> Its stately branches and delicately laced limbs
>   startled me.
> 'Where have you been?' I said.
>   'Or better yet,
> Where have I been
>   That I should just now begin to see?' "

And then it was gone. The darkness settled in, and I moved back toward my bed to begin again trying to make out the strange shapes and sounds of my own black world.

A depressed person needs desperately to hear himself.

Someone was needed to help me interpret the sights and sounds of that foreign world.

Many times my family tried. I would tell them how I felt, or what I was thinking. But often my feelings were so crazy and my thoughts so bizarre that to attempt to describe them was too threatening for any of us to grapple with.

It was during one of these brooding moments that Emery moved back into my life.

I was in Isla Vista, California, resting and recovering, when he called. I hadn't seen Emery for years. We had driven cross-country together and shared college experiences. He had been a student in my wife's speech class.

Since moving into the ever-busy world of Christian ministry, we had seen each other only on rare occasions.

"This is Emery," he said. I responded with a guarded, "Oh . . ."

"How are you feeling, Don?"

Ignoring his question, I asked, "Who told you I was here?"

"Bob Gillikin," he said.

Emery had a totally disarming manner. A quiet but genuine compassion graces his voice whenever he speaks. His questions are always asked with compelling concern. I felt myself relaxing as we talked.

"May I take you to lunch?" he asked.

"No." The answer was immediate and final. No explanation, no apology—just, "No."

After a few more moments we hung up.

I felt that I had been spared an unwanted intrusion into the privacy of my black hole.

He called again the next day, asked the same question, and received the same reply.

He called again and again until he finally caught me in a moment of deep loneliness. I agreed to have lunch with him.

I had no idea what to expect. Numerous times I was tempted to call and cancel. At other times I looked forward to seeing him with enthusiasm, even excitement.

As we sat across the table from each other, I sensed no distance, no judgmental spirit, I heard no clichés, he shared no profound truths—he just listened without comment.

When he was convinced that I had said all I was going to say, he told me about the time he was depressed. His depression, in many respects, bore a marked resemblance to mine.

He also told me of his wife's nervous breakdown. For years she had been unable to be the wife and mother she had so wanted to be.

He mentioned the time he, too, had felt "thrown away" by a church family to whom he had ministered.

After bringing me up to date and telling me of his continued schooling, his doctor's degree in counseling, and his current counseling practice, he asked, "May I be of help to you, Don?"

"No," I replied. "I'll be all right."

Inwardly my soul was crying out for someone who would listen—someone who could listen without responding—without judging. Someone who could help me translate the meaningless jumble of scrambled thoughts without taking offense or being critical.

I was too closed, too masked, too threatened. I had never really bared my soul to anyone, not even myself. I was so afraid to take it out and look at it that again I slammed the lid shut and guarded it with all the emotional strength I had at my disposal.

Emery then told me a story.

"A man was walking in a wilderness. He became lost and was unable to find his way out. Another man met him. 'Sir, I am lost, can you show me the way out of this wilderness?' 'No,' said the stranger, 'I cannot show you the way out of this wilderness, but maybe if I walk with you, we can find our way out together.' "

There was a long silence as he let those words sift down through the unguarded cracks in my defenses. Finally, from somewhere deep within came a desperate cry for help. "Please, Emery, walk with me."

Each night I went to his home after his counseling schedule was finished. I felt great guilt, intruding on the few sacred moments Emery and Mary Ann had together, but I never sensed that I was an imposition.

My fragile spirit could not have suffered any rejection. Had I been made to feel unwanted or even unexpected, I would have flown, never to return.

Two illusions were shattered during the long hours that followed:

> 1. *That counselors are unnecessary in the Christian life.*

I had believed this, even ridiculed the counseling profession at times.

Jourard discovered that no man can really know himself until he has been able to verbalize himself to someone he can trust. [1]

King David often employs this therapy in the Psalms as he verbalizes his transient feelings to God.

> 2. *That if I ever really got in touch with my true self, all I would find would be a hideous monster.*

As I pulled back the curtains and allowed Emery and myself a peek at the inner man, I was both delighted and relieved. Most of my thoughts had no basis in fact whatever—they were just feel-ings—they were emotions running wild and unchecked. Or they related to some past transaction that had never been satisfactorily completed.

Emery is still my counselor. He still reminds me not to be-lieve everything I think or feel. Occasionally, when the darkness settles in, he is still available to walk with me.

Chapter 4, Notes

[1]Sidney M. Jourard, *The Transparent Self,* 2d ed. (New York: Van Nostrand Reinhold Co., 1971).

*"My loved ones and my friends stand
aloof from my plague;
And my kinsmen stand afar off."*
Psalm 38:11

Chapter 5

Withdrawal

*P*art of the admission procedure included the processing of certain forms and the storage of whatever valuables a person chose to bring to the hospital with him.

I waited in line, oblivious to my surroundings, until a familiar feminine voice said, "Next."

I knew that voice. I knew it well. I had preached to that voice, prayed with that voice, cried with that voice; the voice that had penetrated my silence was the voice of one of my sheep—my "family"—my church members.

In the split micro-second that it takes for two pairs of eyes to meet I wanted to dissolve—to disappear—to die—anything but to be forced to greet one of my own while being ushered through that heavy steel door into Ward 7E.

I watched as disbelief flashed across her face. "Pastor," she said, "what are you doing . . . ." and her voice trailed off into nothingness as awareness finally displaced her confusion.

The conversation went nowhere. It never ended. It never really began. There was just this weak greeting—and then nothingness.

We both finished our work quickly and withdrew. I into my deep humiliation and she into her utter disbelief.

What do sheep do when the shepherd is disabled?
Just as they do with anyone else who's ill—
They pray
They write
They call
They visit
UNLESS—
That someone is mentally ill.

We often say that everyone feels clumsy in the presence of grief. Yet in the presence of mental illness, we're all total cripples.

I have never felt so deserted in all my life. For seven years I had given my time, my energy, my love, and all the abilities I possessed to a wonderful church family. And yet in my deepest need, they were unable to respond.

Unable—not unwilling. Church families are just like human families. It's easy to tend to wounds that are visible and pray for ailments that are definable, but mental illness still carries with it the stigma of the dark ages. The Christian community really hasn't advanced very far when it comes to ministering to the depressed.

The interactions between the depressed and those he loves most are terribly baffling.

As I began to withdraw, first from my wife, then my children, and eventually from my church family, not wanting to impose my unhappiness on them, they began feeling, not compassion, but rejection.

The further I withdrew, the greater was that feeling of rejection.

Prior to being hospitalized, I'd take long drives in the car or long periods of rest away from home. The church would graciously extend periods of time away from my work. I'd often sleep alone.

Whenever I was unable to preach, yet well enough to attend church, I would never go to my own. I longed for anonymity.

As I withdrew, the conclusion of my loved ones was often that I no longer loved them. I no longer cherished their company. I no longer desired their fellowship.

In reality, just the opposite was true. I loved them too much to inflict my darkness upon them. My moods and my responses were so unpredictable I feared that in one weak moment a cherished relationship might be destroyed forever.

In the last meeting that I attended with my board of deacons, I suddenly and unpredictably lashed out at one whom I deeply loved. To this day, I'm sure he does not understand—nor do I.

Another response to my depression was that in some way or other my family or my church felt responsible for the great gloom that had settled upon me. This caused feelings of guilt. Many times when I would retreat into silence, Martha would ask, "What have I done?"

One of my former church members who did write, said, "Please tell us what we did wrong."

Feelings of rejection and feelings of guilt only compounded the problem. They created greater distance. They eventually made communication not only difficult, but at times impossible.

My children were convinced that they and they alone were the authors of every one of my bad moods.

Try as I might, it was impossible to convince my wife, my son, my daughter, and my church that I deeply loved them and that what was happening to me had nothing whatever to do with them.

Yet, those I loved the most continued to stagger between feelings of rejection and guilt. They felt either responsible or not wanted.

These persistent feelings were compounded by the fact that there seemed to be no apparent reason for my depression. When the reason for depression is well-defined and clearly understood, there is little cause for confusion. But my "moments" would come without any advance warning and oftentimes during periods of great happiness.

It is impossible for those who have never been depressed to fully understand the deep, perplexing pain that depression causes.

I appeared healthy, without bandages and without crutches. There were no visible scars, no bleeding, and yet there was that endless, indefinable pain that no doctor's probing finger could locate—no drug could totally relieve. There was always the pain and along with it always the desire for oblivion—an oblivion that would come only in minute snatches of restless sleep.

Some of my most consoling moments came when I sensed I was in the presence of someone who really understood how badly I hurt.

Most of my "comforters" were terribly impatient with me. Many of these felt compelled to finish the slow-moving sentences that I tried to speak. Many found it difficult to slow their pace to mine. Even my steps had become halting. Some told me to "pull myself together" and others could not understand why I could not get up and get moving.

Only one could sit beside me for those seemingly endless moments of silence when nothing would come and nothing needed to.

I looked forward so much to those daily visits.

Martha usually came alone—usually in the early evening—and always brought with her the positive cheer that never ignored my pain but always refused to submit to it.

Just a week after my admission to Ward 7E, I wrote in my diary: "Martha was back this evening. We went out on the lawn for more than an hour—delightful time. Martha is wonderful to talk with. If this is the only plus benefit of this entire experience, it will be well worth it."

A depressed person's family must learn quickly to find its balance on the tightrope between rejection and guilt. In most cases, the family is not the cause of the depression and in most cases the depressed person's withdrawal is not to be viewed as rejection.

If he must withdraw—let him go. Let him move in whatever direction he chooses without encumbering him with guilt. His wanderings will be carefully monitored by the Holy Spirit, and his return will be hastened by the very fact that you respected his moods sufficiently to let him go.

Let him express his ambivalence without giving too much credence to some of his foolish statements. He may say to his children, "I hate you," or to his wife, "I want a divorce." At the moment he makes those statements he may genuinely feel them; but his feelings, remember, are transient and unpredictable and are subject to wide swings that ultimately come back into balance.

Pray positively. Philippians 1:6 provides a positive promise that enables us to constantly thank God in advance for His divine provision. When you pray with a depressed person, your prayer might well include such statements as, "Thank You, Father, for Your presence. Thank You that You're here even if it doesn't feel like it. Thank You that this depression is going to lift and life is going to come into focus again. Thank You, Father."

For you can be assured—it will.

". . . curse God and die!"
Job 2:9

Chapter 6

Death Wish

*M*y first morning in Ward 7E was spent in a suicide-prevention class. It was there I learned that deep, long-lasting, chronic depression often ends in suicide. Suicide is the tenth leading cause of death in America, second for college-age students, and third for adolescents. Suicide now ranks as the fifth largest killer in the fifteen to fifty-five age group.

The typical American suicidal is a white, Protestant male in his forties, employed, and the father of two children.

Dr. Bertram Brown,[1] Director of the National Institute of Mental Health, has stated that of those who have clearly committed suicide, it is found that over 80 percent were definitely depressed. One of the most common things that occurs prior to suicide is depression.

Dr. Whyte singled me out as the newest candidate for his probing series of questions designed to prevent suicide.

"Ever thought of committing suicide?"
"Yes."

"What method would you employ?"
I resisted this question. Not that I had not already decided upon a method, but I had never before divulged it.

47

Hesitantly I answered, "I'd shoot myself."

"With what?"

"A .22 calibre revolver."

"Do you own a .22 calibre revolver?"

"Yes."

"Where do you keep it?"

"In a drawer."

"Is it loaded?"

"No."

"How would you do it?"

"I'd just shoot myself."

"No," he said, "that's not what I mean. In what way would you shoot yourself? Would you place the gun in your mouth—to your head, or point it at your heart? How would you do it?"

The process of verbalizing these prior thoughts was difficult but it was already forcing me into a reality consciousness that I had never allowed myself to consider.

Slowly I answered, "I would shoot myself in the head."

"In what room?"

Again with painful hesitance I answered, "In the bedroom."

"Whose bedroom?"

"My wife's and mine," I said.

"Where in the bedroom?"

"Probably on my side of the bed, next to the window."

"What time of day?"

I was hating him with each new question. He was exposing the deepest recesses of my mind to myself and to that group of men. I wanted to scream at him. I wanted to run from him. But he persisted, "What time of day?"

"Probably in the afternoon—my worst time—when the family is gone."

"Who would be the first to find you?"

I hadn't thought this far. Slowly the vision of a bright-eyed, happy-faced eighth grader, arms full of school books, walking down the street, her best friend by her side, came into focus. I could hear her as she skipped up the steps, slid open the door, and hollered, "Dad, I'm home."

He asked it again, "Who would be the first to find you?"

I lowered my head and said her name—"My daughter—my princess—my Kathy."

Without a pause he asked, "What would her reaction be?"

I tried to imagine her shock, her fright, her disbelief, her frightened attempts to help, her screams, her utter feeling of helplessness and despair. "She'd cry."

"Who would she blame?"

It was not difficult to answer this question. Hundreds of times I've watched different degrees of marital disintegration and numerous times I've seen the aftermath of a crushing suicide experience. Inevitably the living never blame the dead—they blame the living—they blame themselves. Kathy, whose only contribution to my depression had been to continue to love and pray for her daddy—who had written love notes and poems to encourage her daddy—would blame herself.

"Who would be the next to find you?"

By this time—I was pleading with him to stop. "In just a moment," he said. "I think you've had enough. Just answer my last question, 'Who would be next to find you?' "

"John, my son, as he came home from school."

"What would his reaction be?"

"Disbelief," I said. "Disappointment, deep uncontrolled grief that would probably display itself in frustration and anger."

"Sons tend," he said, "to follow the examples of their fathers. I would expect, Mr. Baker, if at some time in your son's life things got too difficult for him, that he would take his life, just as his father had done. Self-destruction often breeds self-destruction," he said.

"The purpose of suicide is usually to destroy the hated self and to end all suffering. In reality, however, suicide is an intensely selfish act, destroying not only the one who takes his life, but planting the seeds of destruction in the lives of all who loved him."

Without my realizing it, these penetrating questions were being used to determine the degree of risk involved in my own suicidal thoughts.

Several strong predictive signs suggested that the risk factor was high and there was the real danger that risk could become reality.

1. I had developed a specific plan with a lethal means which was readily available to me.
2. I had given thought to the possibility almost daily and had even threatened it to others.
3. I was suffering a deep and interpersonal loss and felt cut off from my most important social resources—my family, my home, and my church.
4. My future was bleak. I could see no opportunity for recovery to the ministry.
5. My expectations were unrealistic. I could find no other word than "failure" to describe my present state.
6. I fit the profile—white, Protestant, male in his forties, employed, and the father of two children.

And yet that little trip we had just taken through the door of threat into the room of reality had caused something significant to happen. In just a few minutes' time the word "suicide" had lost its appeal. For what had at one time seemed like a viable means of escape had now taken on the appearance of a monstrous catastrophe.

Dr. Whyte suggested some methods of prevention:

1. It must be recognized that depression may be a fatal illness, terminating in self-destruction.
2. Every expressed death wish must be taken seriously.

I recall the time, one Saturday afternoon, when I was called to the home of a deeply depressed mother. Her husband had deserted her, and her sons were out of control. I found her sitting in the middle of her bed, frantically pulling the trigger of her husband's revolver, unaware that the cylinder had been removed. On numerous occasions she had dropped hints—hints that should have been taken seriously. Her life was spared, but not because of an alert pastor—only because a lethal weapon had been wisely dismantled.

    3. Remove all lethal weapons and drugs.

    4. Expect that even Christians will commit suicide.

A young man in my church received Christ on Sunday, shared an exciting testimony on Wednesday, and shot himself on Thursday. His depression had so fully invaded his life that it took only the slightest discouragement to push him back down into the depths where, in utter despair, he took his life.

    5. Stay with the deeply depressed person until professional help has been secured.

    6. View any significant change in behavior with suspicion. Oftentimes a suicidal person will become relaxed and display normal behavior. The reason may well be that he has made his final decision to die.

Chapter 6, Notes

[1]Bertram Brown, "What You Should Know about Depression," *U.S. News & World Report*, September 9, 1974. Interview copyrighted by *U.S. News & World Report*.

"Why are you in despair, O my soul?
And why are you disturbed within me?"
Psalm 43:5

Chapter 7

"Are You Mentally Ill?"

F ollowing the suicide prevention class I was taken into a small conference room where I met the members of the psychiatric staff. Two men and three women. There was not a word of greeting— no smile—not even an indication that I had entered the room.

Everyone seemed preoccupied with reams of paper work piled high on the conference table.

Finally one of the members nodded in the direction of a chair, and I sat down. The silence continued. I shifted uneasily from one side of the chair to the other until one of the staff members picked up a folder, leafed through it quickly, looked up at me, and said,

"Are you Donald Baker?"

"Yes."

"Are you embarrassed to be here?"

"Yes."

"Is your wife embarrassed?"

"Yes."

"Are you mentally ill?"

I lifted my head slightly to look into the impassive eyes of my inquirer. I don't know what I expected to see as I studied her expressionless face.

Maybe I'd hoped that she already had the answer to that question or quite possibly it had been asked only in half-hearted humor. Maybe it was just rhetorical or hypothetical.

I waited for her to continue, but there was only silence. In desperation I looked from one face to the other in the vain hope that someone would come to my rescue. After what seemed an eternity, the question was asked again,

"Mr. Baker, are you mentally ill?"

My response was undoubtedly a classic study in ambivalence.

With great hesitancy I said, "I don't know," and then retreated slightly into, "I hope not." Fearing the inevitable psychological exposure that I had always resisted, I then said firmly and emphatically, "No!" The silence prevailed. No one spoke. Finally I heard a weak, resigned voice originating from somewhere down deep in my soul, utter a halting and barely audible, "Yes."

I felt that I had just confessed to the unpardonable sin. There was some slight relief in my admission but the overpowering emotion was that it was now time for the gavel to fall. My sentence was about to be pronounced. Punishment was now to be imposed.

Instead, my questioner, with a softening look of compassion, said, "How would you like us to be of help to you while you're here?"

With a deep sigh of unexpected relief I answered, "I really don't know." Then through long and ponderable moments I attempted to explain what I had been longing to hear for nearly four years. "Please," I said, "just tell me how to get out of this black hole I'm in. Please. Please."

Without the slightest hesitancy she answered, "We will. Don't worry, we will. It may take a little time, but we will.

"But first," she continued, "we must determine why you're in this black hole of yours.

"Depression," she went on to explain, "has a cause. It's not the result of some mysterious visitation of the gods. It's an illness that is the result of certain biologic or social forces that in some complex way are acting detrimentally to your health.

"We must find those forces. They may be internal, they may be external. They may be physical, they may be mental. They may be real or they may be imagined, but we must find them and when we do, we will recognize them and so will you.

"Then, Mr. Baker," she said, "you will get better."

I had been searching for the cause of my depression for years.

At first I became almost psychoanalytical. I called it "My Trip to the Womb." I tried to recall all of the early incidents that could possibly have had negative impact.

I remembered hearing of my mother's initial rejection of me at birth. My parents had lost twin girls at ages one and two. These daughters had been replaced by two sons. When I was born my mother was desperately hoping that I would be a girl. At birth, I'm told, she refused to see me—for a full minute or two. This incident had apparently caused little damage to my fragile psyche, since it had often been told as one of the family's longstanding jokes—and I had enjoyed telling it as much as anyone.

I strained to recall the many experiences of discipline in my early life. Both my father and mother had been involved in numerous instances of corporal punishment. These had apparently not traumatized me, for I could recall many more times when I should have been spanked but wasn't.

I walked through the halls of my first and second grade classrooms. I revisited the old homeplaces. There were twenty-three of them. Yes, we moved a lot and possibly the absence of a place to put down my roots had affected me; but when I was growing up, it seemed that many families moved a lot. I never remember resisting or regretting those moves. They seemed to be always exciting to me.

Had I married the wrong girl, chosen the wrong profession, moved to the wrong church? No, none of these could be given much credence. I give God far more credit than this. A sovereign God had delightfully superintended all the major decisions of my life; and time coupled with years of affirming experience had confirmed that these major choices had been the right ones.

Was my family depressive? Some of them, yes—others, no.

Our family had grown up with a work ethic, however, which had made us all terribly conscientious, even compulsive. This work ethic has always been one of the prime suspects in my attempts to determine the cause of my depression.

One psychiatrist went so far as to suggest that my father had been terribly cruel in imposing such a demanding work ethic upon his children.

Twice during extended hospital stays I was given the Minnesota Multiphasic Personality Inventory, a battery of questions that determine one's psychological makeup. In each instance it had indicated some wide gaps between my goals and my physical, intellectual, and emotional abilities to achieve them.

I have always set high goals for my life. I have always wanted to be Number One. I've worked harder, stayed up later, studied longer, in an effort to gain that superiority in my profession. Carnal as it may sound, I've always wanted to be the greatest. "Sanctified ambition," I called it.

At the same time that I had these aspirations, I lacked the robust health, self-discipline, and keen intellect necessary to achieve such goals.

This frustrated me terribly.

I had fully expected that my pastoral experience was going to launch me into heights of meteoric accomplishment.

As this goal became more elusive and my attempts to reach it more demanding, I found myself mentally retreating into a rather strange and forbidding world. I began feeling depressed.

I never reached that goal. Others who did began appearing as competitors, even enemies. I deeply resented their successes.

Attempting to achieve success can be terribly depressing in the ministry. A carnal goal can only be accomplished with carnal methods. Carnal methods meant dependence upon human strategy, programing, manipulating, and physical energies—none of which I had in sufficient amounts.

One of my members reminded me one day that "there are only three persons in the Godhead and you are not one of them." My actions had very subtly denied this reality, however, and oftentimes I had suggested by my demeanor that I was all-wise, all-powerful, and ever-present.

What a delightful day it was when I learned that only God is adequate for ministry.

And such confidence we have through Christ toward God. Not that we are adequate in ourselves to consider anything as coming from ourselves, but our adequacy is from God (2 Corinthians 3:4-5).

As I was attempting to unravel the complex implications of success and faithfulness, I came into the possession of a series of cassette tapes used to record a teaching session by Dr. Ray Stedman. The passage being studied was 2 Corinthians 2-6. These discussions later formed the basis for his book entitled *Authentic Christianity*—a must for anyone who desires to serve God effectively.

I'll be eternally in the debt of Dr. Stedman, because the fresh biblical concepts in these oft-neglected passages changed my life and ministry.

They helped considerably to bring this conflict into focus.

There's a fine line between compulsion and sanctified ambition. It has taken years to discover it, and maintaining a balance is oftentimes like walking a tightrope.

The scriptural requirement for a good steward is faithfulness, not success. Faithfulness *is* success, regardless of how it may appear in the eyes of this world.

These truths released me, freed me, and enabled me to place my confidence where it belonged and in so doing caused me to leave the outcome of my efforts where they belonged—with God.

"I was dumb and silent,
I refrained even from good;
And my sorrow grew worse.
My heart was hot within me;
While I was musing the fire burned; . . . "
Psalm 39:2, 3

Chapter 8

Group Therapy

*B*ut I was still depressed.
   A strange mixture of feelings prevailed whenever I found myself scheduled for group therapy in Ward 7E.

I looked forward to the therapy sessions with a restrained excitement, combined with a feeling of frightening apprehension.

Excited over the prospect that some question might be asked, or some statement might be made, that would cast light down into my black hole . . . apprehensive with the fear that someone would strip away one or more of the many masks I had accumulated during my years of public life.

One counselor, David, could probe our minds with the superb skill of a surgeon. More than once I watched him as he began a particularly brutal line of questioning. After long minutes of emotional pain, he was able to help one of us gain an insight that ultimately became a source of slight relief.

Most of the people in my group were young, just released from active military service, and had been involved with drugs. Many of the users had become addicted to drugs or were helpless alcoholics. Vietnam was the recent tour of duty for a good number of them.

Their struggles were immense. Mine seemed terribly mild by

comparison.

One young man had returned from Vietnam a psychological cripple. His mood swings would take him from the extremes of deep depression to acts of insane violence.

He had accidentally killed some Vietnamese children.

The counselor had been working with him for months, trying to help him gain release from the overpowering sense of guilt that bound him. David finally persuaded him to verbally relive those tragic moments in "Nam." We listened spellbound as he painted a grim word picture of the scene that smoldered in his mind.

When finally he had said it all and had left us mentally staring at the lifeless corpses of innocent children, he began to cry. The convulsive sobs that followed wracked his entire body.

No one moved to comfort him. No attempt was made to quiet him; we all sat mute and still.

Finally, as his crying began to subside, David said quietly, "And you feel that you need to be punished for what you did?" The young veteran began nodding his head and saying, "Yes, yes . . . I need to be punished. Yes, yes."

To my utter amazement, David moved from his chair, picked up a wooden ruler, and said, "Hold out your hands." As the ex-soldier obeyed, the therapist began beating his hands and his forearms mercilessly.

I expected just token punishment—a symbolic beating. But David didn't stop, and we recoiled as we saw that ruler come down again and again on hands that began reddening and swelling with each successive blow.

After what seemed an eternity, the beating ended. The tears gone, the look of pain had eased. Our counselor took that grown man in his arms and held him close as a father would his son, all the time repeating, "It's all right. It's all right. It's over. It's over."

The rest of us then crowded close and held that Vietnam veteran until he began to relax. He looked at the therapist and then at the rest of us and began to sob in relief, uttering over and over again, "Thank you, thank you."

Diane was another therapist I encountered who was skilled at helping her subjects find relief.

I respected her for her confrontive abilities which drew all of us out of our protective shells. But at the same time I resented the verbal manner in which she dealt with patients.

Her language, to me, was unbearable. The gutter talk, the four-letter words, the explicit phrases that passed from client to therapist and back again, cut through me like a knife. I was so conscious of this foreign language that it took me days to penetrate beyond it, to see and hear the meaningful transactions that were taking place in the lives of many group members.

She occasionally worked with me, but seldom did we have a significant exchange. I did learn, however. In fact, one of the most profound insights I gained was a result of her group therapy session.

I wrote in my diary, "Diane is trying to get me to be a more aggressive person. She is not succeeding." As I reflected on those words, a little light came on; and I added, "I cannot be aggressive until I become angry, then hostility takes over and eventually I am completely immersed in guilt."

This was a pattern of life for me. Somehow I had gained the impression that confrontation, directness, and even argumentation were not Christian.

I had never learned to rationally express disagreement or displeasure.

Whenever I encountered a disagreeable experience in the hospital, I suppressed it until eventually I could suppress it no longer. And it would then burst from within in the form of hostility.

Punishment of my children was usually done in anger. This was probably one of my greatest sources of guilt.

I would allow anger to seethe until its source was no longer definable. This floating anger would then lash out unpredictably in any or every direction and usually land on unsuspecting—even innocent—victims.

The ensuing guilt would devastate me. No matter how many times the victim would offer forgiveness, I could never forgive myself.

Feelings of guilt are quite often the cause of depression.

None of us can break God's rules, society's rules, or even our own set of rules, without feeling the pain of guilt.

Guilt is a subjective human response to what is viewed to be sin. It is one of God's ingenious tools designed to painfully penetrate the soul of humanity in order to drive humanity to the only adequate provision for sin, which is Jesus Christ.

David in Psalm 32 gives us a classic description of depression resulting from human guilt. He describes the physical and emotional responses by saying,

> When I kept silent about my sin, my
>   body wasted away
> Through my groaning all day long.
> For day and night Thy hand was
>   heavy upon me;
> My vitality was drained away as with
>   the fever heat of summer (Psalm 32:3-4).

This was how I felt when my responses were ugly and un-Christian. The ugly words that spewed from my mouth left me drained of all vitality as I floundered in my black hole.

My problem was not just anger, with its subsequent guilt, or hostility. It was also a problem in communication. I had never learned to disagree agreeably.

I began forcing myself to learn to respond to every question and to question every response. I struggled for clarification. Often I would repeat another's statement before responding, to be sure its meaning was clear.

I would not allow myself to brood over ambiguity. I repeatedly asked for meaning whenever meaning was hidden or uncertain.

I began working to express disagreement before disagreement could deteriorate into hostility.

Learning to share myself at the appropriate time and in the appropriate manner meant that I was to become more bold, more direct, more confrontive and sometimes even more blunt.

My first attempts at this were very clumsy. It's not easy to learn ". . . to speak the truth in love" (Ephesians 4:15). Oftentimes

I moved to the extremes of cruelty and insensitivity. But I found it necessary to carefully analyze all feelings as well as all responses before I wrapped words around them.

Some of my feelings today are just as irrational and senseless. But in verbalizing them I literally defuse them and ultimately render those emotional time-bombs harmless before they are allowed to scatter verbal debris in all directions.

This insight, though it offered no immediate relief, was to later become profound and meaningful, especially in the pulpit.

Many times I have "vented" from the pulpit, overreacting to some trivial, unimportant event, not realizing that my reaction was not to the stated event at all. It was often to some unresolved inner conflict of my own that had needed careful attention.

To be able to carry only one package at a time into the pulpit—one truth—without being forced to juggle it with undetected emotions, has turned preaching into a pleasurable, non-threatening experience.

This insight did not show me the way out of my black hole, but I'm convinced that it has often kept me from falling back in.

"My tears have been my food day and night,
While they say to me all day long,
'Where is your God?' "
Psalm 42:3

Chapter 9

Has God Deserted Me?

O ne of my early callers was a well-meaning Christian who made weekly visits to Ward 7E.

I tried to avoid him; nevertheless, he recognized me, called me by name, and then tried vainly to stammer some words that wouldn't betray his shock at finding a Christian minister in a psychiatric ward.

Before leaving, he asked if he could pray with me. Included in his prayer were the words, "Father, forgive this man for whatever sin has brought him here. . . ."

There were other words included in his prayer, I'm sure, but none penetrated, for suddenly my mind had absorbed all it could hold.

After he left, I buried my head in a pillow and sobbed until there were no tears left in me. "Please, Father," I cried, "tell me what I need to do! Please, Father, just tell me something."

But the heavens were silent—or so it seemed.

For hours each day I would ponder such questions as:

"Where is God?"

"Why doesn't He answer me?"

"Has God really deserted me?"

My theology rejected the last possibility, but my life seemingly had nothing to show for His abiding presence.

My Bible kept saying to me that God is a changeless God, and yet it seemed that without explanation He suddenly had become terribly indifferent.

This God of mine, who had promised never to leave or forsake, appeared now to be playing some cruel form of hide and seek. No matter how diligently I sought Him, He was nowhere to be found.

This God whom I had loved and served had promised to keep His ears ever open to my cries. When I prayed, however, it seemed that He had now become stone deaf.

My Bible, always a source of strength, had little to say to me. When it did speak, the words were soon lost in the pall of gloom and forgetfulness that had settled down over my mind.

Time and again I would leaf through its pages, seeking a promise or an explanation, only to close its covers in disappointment.

Martha brought me a book by Andrew Murray, one of my favorite authors, entitled *Abiding in Christ*. The cover picture was that of an earnest Christian kneeling beside a chair, apparently agonizing in prayer.

I studied the picture for a few moments and then threw the book across the room in disgust.

In later years that same book became a treasure, but often I have recalled that moment with bewilderment, wondering what emotion triggered such a violent response.

Was I expressing a momentary disbelief in prayer?

Was that picture calling on me to expend levels of energy which I no longer possessed?

Was the whole concept of "abiding" saying something to me that I wasn't ready to hear?

I have never known for sure just why I threw that little book with such force—except that possibly the word *abide* had never been one of the more important words in my theological system. The word really had very little meaning—relational significance for sure, but its experiential meanings were vague and elusive.

To "abide" had always meant something similar to "stop," to

"rest," to "be still," to "be quiet."

Whenever I would read a verse like Psalm 46:10, "Be still (cease striving) and know that I am God," I would never stop to ponder its meaning.

Christian ministry, to me, was never characterized by words like *rest, stop, quiet,* or *stillness*. If that was what abiding meant, I didn't have time to waste on such an exercise.

For twenty years I had grown accustomed to a ministry of action—a ministry that made insistent demands on both time and energy. I was convinced that I should be in my study before the men of my church began their work day. I prided myself on being the last to turn out my light at night.

In three pastorates I gave my entire work day to counseling and visitation—six days each week. After the family would retire, I would slip over to my office to spend the quiet hours of the night in study, returning home at about four in the morning.

This schedule worked well until some of the local police officers came to Christ. Those officers who worked the night shift would drive by, see my light on, stop, and come in for counseling.

I was accustomed to a Christianity that gave obvious active meaning to every moment. Anything less suggested a flaw in my commitment.

Friends would encourage me to slow down. Doctors would warn me to change my lifestyle.

Encounters with God were always on the run. Prayers were telegraphed.

My study of Scripture was impersonal. Every new concept was assimilated with my people in mind and remembered only to be incorporated into a future sermon.

For a fast-paced Christian like myself, the word "abide" had little meaning.

Now that my whole world had stopped its violent, wrenching pace—I was bewildered.

Like Elijah (1 Kings 19:10-12) I felt that I had been exceptionally zealous for the Lord. I had worked diligently at tearing down the "false altars" to the "false gods." I was accustomed to the "great and strong winds" and the "rending of the mountains" and the "fire" and the "earthquakes," but a total stranger to the "still small voice."

There comes a time in every Christian's life when the only thing he can do is "abide."

My time had come and I did not know how to do it.

It took weeks for an active mind to slow to the pace of an exhausted body. When it did, however, I was pleasantly surprised.

God was still speaking—

God was still present—

His Spirit had not flown—

His power had not diminished.

I had stopped. God had not. In the quietness God had unique methods available to say things to me—some things I had never taken time to hear before.

Through the lips of friends, on little get well cards, in seemingly insignificant events, God kept whispering sweet somethings to my heart.

I finally opened my Bible again. During the last few weeks in Ward 7E, I spent every private moment studying just four chapters (chapters 13-16) in the Gospel of John. I would have gone farther, but I found it impossible to do so. There was just too much. My Lord had said so much in that Upper Room that I had never really heard before. It was as if I were hearing it for the first time. And it was to me—to me alone—not to my people—just to me. A very private, very wonderful little seminar was being conducted in that little cubicle. The emptiness and loneliness would disappear for a brief time each day.

I found to my amazement that God even loved the inactive. What a revelation! What a delight to just abide.

I found to my amazement that God not only loved me in my inactivity, but He had things to say that could never be heard and understood on the run.

There are times today that I long to return to the stillness of that little room and the joy of that refreshing experience.

My God had not deserted me—just redirected me and then settled down with me to teach me things about our relationship that could never be learned on the spiritual battlefields of life.

". . . he can deal gently with the
ignorant and misguided, since he
himself also is beset with weakness."
Hebrews 5:2

Chapter 10

My Fellow Sufferers

*T*o admit to my fellow patients that I was a minister was terribly embarrassing. I was always grateful to those staff members and patients who didn't probe with the ever-present question, "What do you do for a living?" These were few, however.

Most of these strangers in this other world were very inquisitive. After asking my name, the next question usually was an inquiry into my profession.

I tried desperately to remain detached, withdrawn, and, if possible, anonymous. Of course, I couldn't.

One of my two roommates was the first to know. He was the son of a Bible college professor. But his teenage years had been wasted due to the continual use of drugs and his mind crippled by the abusive chemicals he had injected into his body. Before his admission to Ward 7E, he had been arrested on charges of rape, assault with a deadly weapon, and kidnapping, all accomplished in a twenty-four hour spree of terror. His terror was now confined to our room, where his obscene language and actions escaped the nurses' attention.

I had never bunked with a criminally insane person in my life; likewise, he'd never roomed with a Baptist preacher.

He was assigned to escort me to the lab shortly after my arrival. As we walked down those long, sterile corridors I noticed a look of disdain whenever our eyes met. I finally turned to him and asked, "Why are you looking at me that way?"

"That's the way you're looking at me," he answered.

That was my first rebuke. It was appropriate and timely. I'm thankful now that it came on my first day. I had really never given the subject much thought, but I'm sure that I regarded inmates in mental institutions as "lesser beings." I was inclined to look beyond their personhood and see only their problem.

Fred, another patient, and I met while folding sheets in the laundry room. Fred was twenty-seven, the father of two children. He and his wife were separated.

He had been arrested for drunkenness and indecent exposure and admitted with delirium tremens. His daily nourishment consisted of "bennies" and a half gallon of whiskey.

After telling me his story he asked, "Hey, what do you do for a living?" I was silent for a long time, worried that my answer would create distance between us. Finally I answered him, slowly and reluctantly. "I'm a minister," I said.

His response was immediate and animated. He dropped the sheet he was folding, grabbed my hand, shook it wildly, and said, "Damn, that's great. I've never talked to a preacher before. Tell me, what's it like? What do you do? How does it feel? Do you think I could ever become a Christian?" He never once asked me why I was there.

Bill, who later became a dear friend, was an alcoholic who was in for rehabilitation. His drinking had begun at a housewarming. He and his wife had just finished building a beautiful home in the suburbs. They decided that it would be impolite to invite guests without having liquor available. He prepared a drink for his wife—her first. When she later died from the effects of alcohol, his life disintegrated. He not only was alone and an alcoholic, but also thought himself a murderer. His guilt had driven him to numerous suicide attempts.

Alcoholics have a world of their own, and they cannot believe that there are those who do not drink.

In therapy sessions with alcoholics, the psychiatrist turned to me and asked, "How long have you been an alcoholic?"

"I've never drunk," I told him.

The entire group laughed incredulously. The doctor got up from his chair, walked over to me, and said, "You're a damn liar, and the sooner you admit that to yourself the better off you'll be." To this day, I still doubt that he believes me.

Bill gave me my first lecture on alcoholism and then took both Martha and me to the Alcoholics Anonymous meetings. I had never realized the complexity or the severity of this problem. These men became close friends after I had learned to relax with them. In later weeks most of my spare time was spent in counseling them. They appointed me as their chaplain and asked me to serve as a member of the board of directors for their Halfway House.

Bill gave his life to the Lord and went from the hospital to Bible school to study the Scriptures. He entered his new world very clumsily but with great delight.

He stopped at our home following an afternoon session in class. All four of us were at home. He came into our living room in tight-fitting jeans, western shirt, and boots. He tossed his wide-brimmed hat on the chair and announced, "Hot damn, I just had the greatest time of my life. I just learned about the *crucification*."

Some of the staff members often displayed more hostility than the patients.

I had been instructed to take my medication with food. Pill-taking time required standing in line in front of one of the nurses' "cages" and then swallowing the pills in her presence. When Sheila, a staff nurse, handed me my pills without my snack, I asked her, "Do you really want me to take these on an empty stomach?" She looked at me and snapped, "Have you got someplace else to put them?" I then retreated into my silent world to brood and to mentally create verbal replies designed to devastate her. None of those ingenious retorts was ever delivered. They just sank down into the pit of my stomach and churned.

Chuck, a male nurse, pulled me from my cot on the third morning and said, "OK, Baker, it's time to get up and out. Time to play some softball." With that, he took me to the locked clothes closet, retrieved my street clothes, and told me to put them on.

I wrote in my diary, "It's surprising what a little thing like clothes can mean when you've been denied them, and when they suggested going outside, I felt like turning handsprings.

"But softball? Me—an old man—weak, depressed, playing softball with all those young fellows," I thought.

I complained to Chuck, the male nurse, and spent long minutes describing my health history, my exhaustion, my reluctance. He listened attentively and patiently. After I had finished, he calmly took my hand and said, "OK, now let's go play softball."

Oh, how I hated it at first. Then the need for exercise came into focus. I became aware of the greater opportunity to get better acquainted with the men. It was on the softball field that I accomplished the impossible. I got Harry, my other roommate, who never spoke, never responded, to smile at me.

On my third day at softball I hit a double and then fell from exhaustion before I could reach second base. But oh, what this did for my ego as my new friends cheered me on.

One of the most memorable remarks came from Norm, another staff person who recognized me and had known of my ministry. He played on one of the church softball teams and remembered me from one of the games I had attended.

He took me aside and said, "It took great courage to do what you did!" Those simple words sustained me during those long weeks.

My fellow sufferers became my close friends—a camaraderie developed—much like that acquired in military service.

I find myself to this day defending the unfortunate, the alcoholics, and some of the criminals, and often seeking opportunities to move alongside them.

A call came recently from the psychiatric ward of Portland's Veterans Hospital. I visited a stranger in deep depression who had beaten his wife and children and then attempted suicide. I tried vainly to build a bridge between us. He remained detached and silent until I said, "I think I know how you feel. I've been right where you are—depressed, angry, suicidal. I, too, have served time in a psychiatric ward of a veterans hospital."

With that he looked up in astonishment and said, "You . . . a preacher? I don't believe it." After convincing him, he began to weep. He stood up and threw his arms around me and cried like a baby.

Before I left, he prayed to receive Jesus Christ as his Savior.

"Are you bound to a wife? Do not seek to be released."
1 Corinthians 7:27

Chapter 11

The Family

"*I* think I'd like to have a divorce."
"I don't care what happens to you."
"I don't care what happens to the family."
"I don't care what happens to the church."

It seems impossible that I should speak those words—yet I did. I barely remember them. Martha recalls them vividly.

Those words, common to many, were so foreign to us. Most couples think them at some time, many speak them, some actually mean them.

When I spoke them, they came unexpectedly from somewhere deep in my black world and exploded with powerfully destructive force upon my wife.

Her world was so shattered, so disrupted, and so tentative that she sought counsel from a doctor, a psychiatrist, and from Emery.

During those few hours with Emery she pulled our twenty-three-year marriage out of her memory, studied it carefully, and decided it was worth saving. The love had been genuine, the commitment real, and the memories cherished.

It was primarily because of her refusal to honor my foolish talk that we persisted in working through that very difficult time.

We had met, fallen in love, and married while still in college—she from Indiana, a speech teacher. I, from Oregon, a preacher-boy.

The moment I saw her I fell deeply in love with her. She was all my dreams wrapped up in one person. Flashing brown eyes, long black hair, beautiful features, a petite figure, a sense of determined purpose, strength of character, a love for the Lord, keen intellect, and a desire to marry only a man with whom she could become a soul mate.

I left our first casual meeting, went back to the dorm, knelt beside the bed, and thanked the Lord that He had finally introduced me to my wife.

We were married nine months later.

I often marveled at the faith of a woman whose father was one of the greatest Bible teachers I had ever known and who would marry a preacher whom she had never heard speak.

Ours has been a happy and exciting marriage. We have never known boredom. Living by faith is always an adventure. Each new day is fresh with surprises.

We have always enjoyed happy and fruitful ministries. Our churches have grown, our relationships with our people have always been secure and precious.

We've traveled through much of the world, loving and being loved by a delightful missionary family.

She shares the ministry with me—speaks, counsels, laughs, weeps, and prays with whoever needs her.

Martha is the most accessible person I have ever known—always available to anyone regardless of who they are or what they might need.

I have watched her, perfectly at ease with a railroad bum as she tenderly bandaged his lacerated leg. I have seen her equally composed as she chatted with the President of the United States.

She is a great mother. I never abdicated my role as a parent in favor of the ministry, but there have been many times when she has been forced to be both mother and father and has always performed ably.

Our marriage, like most, however, has had its struggles.

Marriage is designed by God to be part of the perfecting process, and sometimes that perfecting can be terribly painful. At times it has been painful to us.

Our expectations have always been high. We have both refused to settle for mediocrity. Both of us are perfectionists, creative, capable, and competent people, demanding much of ourselves and of each other. There are times, I'm sure, when we subconsciously have even felt in competition with each other.

Our schedules are horrendous. She maintains a career as a speech pathologist, teaches Bible classes, speaks for women's groups, disciples young believers, counsels the hurting, maintains a home, and accompanies me to most of my pastoral engagements. For weeks we may go nonstop, ending each day too tired to talk and sometimes too weary to even pray.

Quite often we're forced to send verbal telegrams to each other or go for long periods of time without really finishing a communicative transaction.

Often I'm gone, and she assumes much of my load as well as her own.

I am not an easy man to live with. Much of the time, even when I'm with her, I'm absent. My mind is busily working through counseling sessions, administrative problems, or preparing messages.

Vacations are cherished times. It's then we laugh and love, walk and talk, and virtually get reacquainted.

To help us bring our marriage back into focus the staff of Ward 7E scheduled a family conference.

I was terrified.

I was certain that I was about to be exposed as the incompetent fraud I felt myself to be. My appraisal of my role as a father, our relationship as a couple, our parenting, was all spelled out in one word: failure. In my darkness I could see nothing that looked good.

The family came, all of them—Martha, John, and Kathy— poised, polite, and beautifully groomed.

The large room with its high windows and bare walls was anything but inviting. The long, wide table forced us to sit uncomfortably far apart. Two staff people whispered to each other, studied a sheaf of papers for a few moments, and then proceeded nervously and very clumsily to penetrate our secret little world.

It was obvious from the beginning that we were somewhat different from the usual clients. There was no alcohol or drug problem. Neither of the children had ever run away from home. No one was scarred from any brutal family beating. The children were not dropouts or truants. The language was not crude or uncaring.

The questions were ill-prepared. We all felt awkward, and yet every question was answered ably and honestly. John and Kathy withheld nothing. Facts as well as feelings were laid out on the table for careful analysis.

"Do your parents love each other?" they were asked.

"Yes," they answered.

"Do they love you?"

"Yes," again.

"Do you love them?"

"Yes," without hesitation.

"Do they ever argue?"

"Yes."

"A lot?"

"More than I want them to," answered John.

"How does that make you feel?"

"We don't like it."

"Does your dad like to have fun?"

"Not much. He's working all the time."

"Do you like your family?"

Both answered "Yes" and seemed surprised that such a question should ever be raised.

It was concluded that our family was normal, happy, loving, open, and unusually close.

I was somewhat surprised. That was not the appraisal from deep within my black hole. It didn't quite fit with the miserable images that I had been conjuring up—but it was delightful to hear.

Through all of its ups and downs our marriage had never been brought into question. We never once doubted the fact that God had uniquely designed us for each other—until I let loose of those strange and shattering words that had been given birth somewhere deep in the blackness.

Depression speaks a totally foreign language at times. As it gropes for meaning, it looks at anything and everything that might be its cause and sometimes draws some very foolish conclusions.

At times I'm sure I felt that our marriage was the cause, and divorce was the cure. That thought was one of the many elusive straws I clutched at. I'm so grateful that both God and Martha always kept pushing it beyond my reach and held it there until the darkness finally lifted.

*". . . to keep me from exalting myself,
there was given me a thorn in the flesh,
a messenger of Satan to buffet me—to
keep me from exalting myself!"*
2 Corinthians 12:7

Chapter 12

Physical, Emotional, or Both?

*T*he medical doctor who examined me upon my admission to Ward 7E questioned me carefully. He mentioned his suspicion that hypoglycemia might be playing a part in my illness.

Hypoglycemia, or low blood sugar, has been related to a long list of symptoms and often acts as a catalyst in bringing emotional disturbances to the surface.

The list includes fatigue, anxiety, depression, and tension. It also includes sweating, weakness, tremor, lightheadedness, unexplained hunger, headache, blurred vision, confusion, incoherent speech, wide mood swings, sudden outbursts of temper, forgetfulness, insomnia, and much, much more.

Low blood sugar sounds like the body needs more sugar. Just the opposite is true, however. What it means is that the body has an intolerance to sugar and other similar carbohydrates because of an oversupply of insulin. The excessive insulin drives the blood sugar down. As the sugar falls rapidly, sometimes below safe levels, the above list of symptoms often occurs.

Rapidly falling blood sugar can affect both the mind and the body. The brain is fueled by glucose and when the fuel supply of glucose, or sugar, is low, the person may notice an inability to think clearly or to concentrate. One can become emotionally upset.

83

Depression, anxiety, paranoia, or any number of emotional responses may occur.

A heated medical debate has continued for years. The focal point of this debate is whether hypoglycemia is a very common or very rare disease.

In my first pastorate I experienced a rapid and unexpected weight gain—sixty-five pounds in less than one year. Whenever I would diet—and it was always a crash diet—I would experience a wide range of frightening symptoms, from migraine headaches to fainting spells.

The first time I ever heard the word *hypoglycemia* was from the lips of a doctor who treated me after church one Sunday morning following a mysterious "collapse."

He said, "You know, Reverend Baker, your symptoms sound like you may have hypoglycemia. What you need to do, whenever you feel weak, is eat a candy bar." I did, and I continued to feel weak. I continued to eat candy bars, and I ballooned. My weight went unchecked and out of control, and with the weight gain came all of the negative feelings toward self a person can have when any part of his life is out of control.

I hated myself.

Yet, no matter what diet I chose, it was impossible to maintain it over any period of time without becoming ill.

For long periods I would live on amphetamines (they were prescribed freely then) until I could tolerate them no longer. To help me sleep, doctors would then prescribe seconal. For years I ping-ponged it between "uppers" and "downers," trying vainly to curb my appetite and then calm down sufficiently to sleep.

The inevitable collapse occurred nearly four years before Ward 7E and the lingering exhaustion and depression made it almost impossible for me to do my work.

I received a long-distance telephone call from another longtime doctor friend, Dr. Richard Saloum, who invited me to come see him. Dr. Saloum had spent five years as staff physician at Dammasch State Hospital and had found numerous patients struggling with emotional symptoms that were related to physical problems.

After extensive tests, he confirmed the diagnosis of hypo-glycemia which had been suspected years earlier.

The intense relief that I felt was immediate. Just hearing that the wide, unpredictable, and indefinable mood swings might be re-lated to physical factors brought me added hope.

To hear a doctor confirm that weight loss for a hypoglycemic is an impossibility without a special diet was more than encourag-ing.

Then came discouragement—I could find no other doctor who agreed with that diagnosis. I noticed that whenever I remained with Richie's prescribed regimen, I felt better; but since no one ac-cepted it, I fell back into my old habits and felt worse.

Numerous times during these four baffling years, I lapsed into unconsciousness, and on three occasions was taken by ambu-lance to a hospital. There was never a conclusive diagnosis.

I shuffled down the long hall of Ward 7E in a state of re-strained hopefulness. That doctor had actually said that he sus-pected hypoglycemia. Most of the doctors and psychiatrists I had seen since Richie's diagnosis had not accepted the part it could have played in my struggle.

I was immediately placed on a six-meal per day regimen con-taining high-protein, low-calorie food with vitamin supplements. This diet was maintained during my entire stay in Ward 7E. For ten weeks I ate on schedule and only the appropriate foods. For ten weeks I watched my weight drop daily, regularly, and predictably. I saw it move right down to that figure that I had expressed earlier as only an impossible dream.

With the weight loss came a corresponding rise in self-esteem.

My mood swings became less severe.

The depression began to lift.

The black hole turned somewhat gray.

I found myself praying more, studying more,
    thinking more lucidly.

One weekend I was given a pass to go home to my family.

Saturday night we indulged ourselves in the Baker tradi-tion—popcorn and lots of it. Sunday we went to the Tropicana, a local restaurant, and ate ice cream. Later that day, I ate a candy bar.

On Monday I wrote in my diary:

"Super low! Depressed, weak, nervous, disoriented."

The unit chaplain suggested that I was grieving.

I concluded that if it was grief, it was caused by an overwhelming sense of failure.

It was not until Tuesday evening that the light came on. I wrote in my diary, "If I have hypoglycemia, then why don't I act like it? I'm convinced that my low was related to my bad eating habits over the weekend. I can't accept hypoglycemia as a condition I have and then ignore the effects of excessive carbohydrates—ice-cream, popcorn, etc."

Weeks after my release from Ward 7E, I received an application for renewal of my pilot's license. Two questions were asked: (1) Have you ever had a nervous breakdown? (2) Have you ever been declared insane?

I didn't know how to answer either of them.

I took the application to the head of the Psychiatric Division and laid it on his desk. "Doctor," I asked, "you're the only one who can answer these two questions. Tell me, what was your final decision as to my problem?"

He picked up my chart, reviewed it briefly, and said, "Don Baker, you have not had a nervous breakdown, nor were you insane. In the ten weeks you were a patient here, we proved to our satisfaction that you do have reactive hypoglycemia."

I have lived with that information for ten years now. Conclusions about depression that include hypoglycemia as a factor are accepted by some and rejected by others. In my situation, I allow for its influences.

It necessitates a dietary regimen that is extremely difficult for me to maintain.

It is aggravated by the large doses of stress that one is forced to take along with the ministry.

Often I eat what I'm not supposed to, and, just as often, I pay the consequences.

In looking back, I believe that my struggle was partly related to this physical area. This doesn't minimize the lessons I was learning in other areas of my life. Yet its discovery provided clues, new clues, for my way out.

It has been a source of contention in discussions with others. It's frustrating, and difficult, when people disagree with me about hypoglycemia's part in my depression.

The sole reason for my depression? No. One factor cannot be isolated from all the others. But physical problems are often interrelated with other battles. With this in mind, I made some corrections, and I profited as a result.

"Do not forsake me, O LORD;
O my God, do not be far from me!"
Psalm 38:21

Chapter 13
My Career Is Over . . .

*M*y church family had been very patient. The leaves of absence, the periods of time spent in the hospitals, and now an extended time in Ward 7F., however, had taken their toll.

Sheep need a shepherd. My church was no exception. The attendance had begun to drop off, the sharp edge of excitement was gone, and the people were almost as bewildered as I.

The chairman of the board had announced, for want of a better diagnosis, that I had had a nervous breakdown.

It seemed in the best interests of the church for me to resign. Each day I would struggle with that decision. In the mornings I would waken with the conviction that today some "sign" from heaven or some divine pronouncement would simplify the decision-making process.

Martha and I would discuss it for long periods of time, but when I would ask, "What should I do?" she would always answer with "that has to be your decision."

Bud McRae, chairman of the board, visited me one evening, and all we talked about was whether or not I should continue.

I finally asked him, "Bud, let's pretend we're in a board meeting, and the members are seated again around that long table. I'm going to poll them by name, one by one, and you are going to tell me how you think they would vote."

I drew their names from my memory and began asking the question, "Do you believe that our pastor should resign?" "Marvin," "Melvin," "Bud," and so on until each member had voted in the manner that had been previously discussed. Only one voted, "No." All the others had stated an unqualified, "Yes." I was stunned. I felt so secure, so convinced that they still wanted me, but I had been wrong. My board overwhelmingly believed that I should go.

Never before had any member or group of members in any of my churches even suggested that my work was finished. I felt the blood drain from my face. My hands renewed their shaking. Beads of perspiration popped out on my forehead as the enormity of that judgment began to penetrate.

"But where will I go?" "What will I do?" Many times I had counseled with the unemployed, prayed confidently with them, and assured them, "Don't worry, God will provide."

Suddenly, I was unemployed—for the first time in over thirty years. In fact, I had started earning my own way in the fifth grade and had not, since then, been without an income.

Martha had returned to school and had secured a master's degree in speech pathology and was already in demand in the county school system. But I couldn't depend on Martha to support me. That was not the way it was supposed to be.

I think for a few brief moments the "man of faith," the "spiritual leader," the "pastor," must have displayed panic, for it was then Bud said, "Pastor, don't worry, we have already decided to pay your salary for six more weeks."

I fell silent. "Six weeks," I thought. "Six weeks, with a boy in college and a girl preparing for high school and a home to pay for and a car," and I began thinking through that long list of commitments. Finally I turned to Bud and said, "Thank you, Bud. You have been a big help to me. I'll write my resignation tomorrow."

I wrote it—painfully—and then called the church secretary to type it and mail it through the channels.

When the call was completed, I slowly placed the receiver back into place, shuffled back to my room, and cried.

I felt empty
I felt deserted
I felt unwanted
I felt thrown away

The church was more than justified in its action, but still that action was totally unexpected.

As I thought through all the implications of resignation, I wavered between staying and going. "I'm sure that a majority of the people want me to stay," I thought. "If I could just take my case to the people, they would reverse that decision." I listed the names of close friends I could call, and I began thinking through devious methods to gain the support of a majority.

But then the consequences of such action began to pass through my mind. I had often said that I would never allow a church to "split" because of me.

I am obsessed with the necessity for a visible, tangible, demonstrable unity with the Body. It is one distinguishing mark that sets the church apart from all other organizations or institutions. The church is the only place on earth where the potential for peace is to be found.

Our church had already been divided too many times. I could not and would not be the cause for another fracture.

I let my resignation stand and took the full responsibility for that decision.

I stated to the church that "due to continuing poor health and an unpredictable future, I feel it is necessary for me to tender my resignation."

As I signed that letter, I was sure that all my previous fears were now confirmed—"A life of normalcy is forever threatened. No church would ever call a man to be its pastor who had spent time in a psychiatric hospital." Those words were written in my diary shortly after my admission; now I was convinced that my ministry was finished.

"O God, Thou art my God;
I shall seek Thee earnestly;
My soul thirsts for Thee,
my flesh yearns for Thee,
In a dry and weary land
where there is no water."
Psalm 63:1

Chapter 14

Starting Again

As I left the hospital, there was no fanfare and no welcoming party. That really was the way I wanted it. In fact, I left without even saying goodbye to the staff or to my many new friends.

I returned home with many helpful insights.

I had

a new compassion for the hurting,

a new strategy in counseling,

a new insight into communication.

I had some memories that would last a lifetime.

I had a confirmed diagnosis,

and I could recognize blood sugar episodes,

and knew what to do about them.

I was more calm, more confident.

I was free of the stress of pastoring.

It was Friday and I had no need to prepare sermons for Sunday.

Yet, I was still weak; I was still confused; and I was still depressed.

The black hole wasn't completely black anymore, but it was still dark enough to make it difficult to see any future or even interpret the present.

And, of course, I was unemployed.

For the first time in my life I began leafing through the classifieds. I even prepared a resumé, but I didn't have the slightest idea where to send it.

I timidly called some friends and asked if they knew of anything. I drove from city to city, just dreaming about possibilities, but not really knowing how to make meaningful contacts.

It was then I heard of an opening in a Christian school. The president was a long-time friend. I was excited as I dialed his number, but dismayed when his secretary told me he was busy. It was much later when I received a call from his assistant. Trying to ask for a job was one of the most difficult things I had ever done. The sentences were clumsy. My responses seemed incoherent. I'm not even sure that he fully understood the purpose of my call.

He did say, however, "If there is any opening, we'll call you." He took my phone number, my address, and hung up. He never called again.

I took my family to a number of different churches without ever feeling at home. It seemed that I was permanently and indelibly marked. Those who knew me were terribly condescending. Some of my pastor friends would meet me at the door and after an embarrassed greeting would turn away quickly, not knowing how to act or what to say.

There were a few, and oh, how precious they were, who seemed to genuinely care. Their presence was like a cool breeze on a parched desert. They not only provided much-needed fellowship, but they bolstered a shattered ego.

What was I going to do? I really wasn't strong enough to do much of anything. But as the weeks and months dragged by, I was feeling not only economic pressure but also the great and insistent desire to be busy again in the Lord's work.

After checking out numerous opportunities, I knew there was only one thing in life for me, and that was the pastorate.

I needed to be alone. I needed to pray. I needed to fast. I needed to seek God's face. I needed to know beyond any doubt that God was still there and that He knew I was still here. The heavens had been silent for too long. I had to hear from God.

My friend and neighbor, Arnie Blesse, loaned me his cabin at Hume Lake. I took only enough food to keep my blood sugar under control and left home for an indefinite period of time.

It was almost impossible for me, yet I climbed to the top of a nearby hill and stood beside a wooden cross where hundreds of young people had given their lives to God.

As I stood there, I began to weep. I realized that God's call to me to preach had not been rescinded. He had not changed His mind. There had been no new directions given, no new commands ordered. I was never told how long when my Lord pointed in the direction of His harvest field. I only knew that all of the present uncertainties had come from some strange source other than my sovereign God. He was not the author of my confusion. I didn't know who was, but I was certain He wasn't.

I knelt beside that cross as others had done and began to pray. It was the longest, most lucid prayer I had prayed in months.

"Oh Father," I said, "I love You and I know You love me—even when my feelings tell me otherwise. I still don't know all that's happening in my life or why, but I do trust You. I do know You have a plan and even though I may never fully understand it, I still trust You.

"Please, Father, let me pastor a church again. I'm not interested in its size or its location. Just give me a dozen people to pastor. I'll earn my own living, if necessary. Please, Father, let me be a shepherd again.

"If there has ever been any doubt about my commitment, Father, I want you to know I'm Yours. I'll do whatever You want."

As I knelt on that mountaintop, I took a stake and drove it into the ground—a strange procedure for me—and then said, "Father, I'm driving this stake as a sign that here, at this place, I've committed my life anew, and it's Yours for as long as You want to use it."

I walked slowly down the mountainside, not feeling much different, except that I had made a statement, not out of necessity or fear, not even out of my anxiety, but out of an overwhelming, lucid desire to be used of God in any way He chose to use me.

"Be of sober spirit, be on the alert.
Your adversary, the devil, prowls about
like a roaring lion, seeking someone to devour."
1 Peter 5:8

Chapter 15

My Final Foe

*A*s I sat in that mountain cabin, reflecting upon the reasons for my lingering depression, I asked myself again, "Was Satan in any way connected with my depression?" This question was asked in various forms time and again during my four years of groping in the darkness. Many were convinced he was. I dismissed them all casually and sometimes even carelessly. I rejected the possibility.

The works of Satan had been relegated to textbooks and history. I preached about him occasionally and truly believed in his existence, but never gave him more than just a passing thought.

My first real introduction to the world of the occult came in Haiti in 1965 when I was introduced to Olipha. His story staggered the imagination.

Olipha had kept his little Haitian village completely under his spell for more than fifty years. Men, women, and children both feared and worshiped him. His word was law. His power was real.

Then it happened. Jesus Christ moved into Olipha's family. His brother became a Christian. Shortly after his conversion he confronted Olipha with the message of salvation. Olipha's response to his younger brother was swift and frightening. He pointed his bony finger at this brand new believer and said, "Within three weeks you will die!"

His brother's response was simply, "Olipha, I am no longer afraid of you—'for greater is He that is in me than he that is in you.' "

Twenty-one days later, to the day, Olipha, the sixty-seven-year-old Haitian witch doctor, bowed his head in the presence of his younger brother, still very much alive, and surrendered his life to Jesus Christ.

Olipha, a preacher of the gospel, stirred my heart with his ringing testimony. I had seen a twentieth-century demonstration of divine power in a classic, clear-cut victory over Satan.

Evidences of satanic activity were abundant. Voodoo, witchcraft, sorcery, animal and even human sacrifice were commonplace. Wherever Satan's power was displayed, however, God's power was proven to be greater.

I returned to my church with a new respect for my enemy. Yet, as I looked for him, it seemed that he was nowhere to be found. There were occasional glib references to him, numerous scriptural indications of his activity, but no real evidence of his presence. It seemed, then, Satan was either in hiding or his activity was far too sophisticated for detection.

In recent years, however, the very doors of hell have been opened, and the masks have been torn from Satan's face. In just a few short years the world has witnessed an open frontal assault by our enemy and his demons that is unparalleled in human history. Satan's blitzkrieg has been successful.

I began studying Scripture very carefully to determine whether or not there might just possibly be some relationship between Satan and my depression.

After all, it had been during a series of sermons on Ephesians 6:10-20 that I had first collapsed—and it had been just a few days after my first personal encounter with a Satanist that I slipped into my black hole.

That was a frightening experience. It happened as I was walking to my room at a conference center where I had been invited to teach for a week.

Standing in my path was a handsome young man, twenty-seven years of age, dressed in army fatigues.

"Is your name Baker, or Barker?" he asked.

"Yes," I replied, "my name is Baker."

"I've been told to talk to you," he said.

His manner was strange and threatening. His voice was flat and colorless. His eyes looked cold and empty. I felt fear as I looked at him.

He came into my room with me, and I asked him to be seated. He said, "No, I'll stand." Then he said, "I must tell you something, but I cannot look at you; and you cannot look at my face." With that he turned to the wall, pressed his head against the wallboard, and began reciting the most bizarre story I had ever heard.

He had been a worshiper and priest of Satan for seventeen years. His devotion to the evil one had taken him all over the country and had involved him in every occult practice known to man. Every twenty-two days he was visited by a demon and driven to unspeakable acts of evil. He hated God. He hated Christ. He hated talking to me, but he was compelled.

During the time that he was describing his life, a very strange thing was happening to me. I could not stay awake. I was listening to the most awesome story I had ever heard: sordid, ugly, and frightening. There were descriptions of orgies, confessions of vile practices, admissions of guilt, and, through it all, I wanted to sleep.

I felt drugged and used every method I knew to remain alert. I pinched, bit, kicked myself. I prayed constantly just to be able to stay awake.

After two hours he suddenly turned on me, his eyes filled with hate, and screamed, "Aren't you afraid of me? Don't you know I can kill you?"

With supernatural calmness I looked into that enraged face and said, "No, you can't, for greater is Christ Who is in me than Satan who is in you" (1 John 4:4).

Instantly he screamed, a hideous high-pitched scream, threw up his arms, and fell to the floor. In uncontrolled rage he began pounding his head on the concrete floor, uttering noises horrible beyond description.

I looked around vainly for help. I called, but no one came. I was alone—alone with a demoniac. Face to face with the enemy for the first time.

"O God, what do I do?" I cried. I knelt beside that writhing human form, placed one hand between his forehead and the concrete and the other on his back. As I stroked his head and shoulders I prayed, "Lord Jesus, deliver this man from Satan." I continued to pray, all the time shielding his head from the floor. "In the name of Jesus, Lord of heaven—Lord of all—I command you, Satan, to come out of this man's body."

If there was a precise formula, I didn't know what it was. I did know that Jesus' name always rang the death knell to the demons in the Scriptures.

After what seemed an eternity, his body began to relax. He stopped jabbering and foaming. I urged him to speak the name, Lord Jesus—Lord Jesus. Each time I said that name he looked at me with pleading eyes and then grabbed his throat and his tongue to indicate that he could not speak.

As I knelt beside him, clutching his body to mine, I prayed again, "Lord Jesus, release this man's tongue, that he may speak Your name." Finally, it happened. His lips began forming words. "Say it," I urged. "Say His name. Say Lord Jesus."

"I can't," he cried.

I prayed again.

Finally he lifted his head, summoned the little strength he had left, and cried, "Lord Jesus."

With those words he slumped to the floor, unconscious.

I covered him with a blanket, rubbed his head, massaged his shoulders and back, and waited for him to revive.

His first words after opening his eyes were, "Lord Jesus." He then raised up, moved to the side of my bed, knelt there, and gave his life to Jesus Christ.

It was just two weeks after my encounter that I lay helpless on my office floor.

I sobbed convulsively as they loaded me into the ambulance and continued crying for days. Every new voice—every soft word—would start me crying all over again.

Since my release from Ward 7E, I had read every book available, every Scripture passage that was written, on the subject of Satan.

If there had been any fault after my Satanist friend's deliverance, it was that of self-glorification. I loved to tell that story. I delighted in the admiring responses. I quickly took the praise to myself. I truly underrated the power of the enemy. Pride engulfed me—and nearly destroyed me.

As I was putting together the pieces of the puzzle, I wrote on a sheet of paper:

"Millions are being influenced, oppressed, and enslaved by the occult. The world is reeling as its prince has begun unleashing his fury in preparation for the final deception (2 Thessalonians 2:9-12).

"The church is feeling his blows. Christians everywhere are falling. I fell, emotionally wounded, bewildered, disoriented, confused, depressed—a casualty of Satan's onslaught."

As I wrote those last few words in the silence of that mountain cabin, I suddenly became aware that my paper was nearly drowned with my tears I began to sob, and I said aloud, "Oh, God, is this what happened to me?"

I moved from the table to the couch, weeping and praying and asking forgiveness. I had underrated my enemy. I had ignored the pleas of Scripture. I tried to fight this great battle without my armor. I had taken God's glory to myself and even claimed a victory in which I had only been a bystander. "O Lord, did I really ignore You? Forget You? O Father, forgive me, forgive me."

I continued to kneel by that couch long after the tears had dried and the prayer was finished.

I noticed as I remained there that things felt different. Nothing ecstatic or noisy. Nothing high-powered or sensational. I just felt different.

As I examined that feeling, I became aware of strength in my limbs, of objects before my eyes. I saw, I felt, I heard. Was it possible? Was the cloud finally gone? Had my world come alive again?

I stood and moved carefully at first. The feeling, the sensations, the awareness, the strength—was it real? Was it back to stay? I began thanking and praising God, singing and laughing.

I put on my shoes and ran down the hillside—more falling than running from Arnie's cabin to where carpenters were building a new dining hall. One of my deacons was there. I shouted to him, "Jerry, I'm all right! Thank you for praying." He looked bewildered and unbelieving. He needed time; but eventually he, too, would rejoice at the reality of what had finally come full circle.

I continued to walk with vigor for the full three miles around the lake. I sang. I cried. I laughed. I prayed. I quoted Scripture. I talked to the birds, I talked to the trees.

To this day I'm grateful no one saw me. I would have been shipped back to Ward 7E for sure.

Three days were spent testing and trying this new view of the world, no longer from within a black hole, but now from a mountain peak where I could see anything, everything, clearly and distinctly. My depression was finally gone with all its multiple causes and multiple effects . . . it was gone.

Upon arriving home, I called my family together and told them nothing—only that God had been working. "I won't explain it for at least three days. In the meantime," I said, "just watch me and listen to me, and see for yourself that I am different."

With that, I went to the garage, cranked up the lawn mower, and proceeded briskly to mow first the front yard and then the back. I edged the lawn, raked up the grass, put away the tools, and strode past three astonished human beings. They had been watching me from the window all the time I had been working, fearful that at any moment they would be forced to come out and pick me up. As I walked back into the house, they asked if I was all right. When I answered, "Yes," they asked me to tell them what was happening. "Not yet," I said. "Let's wait and you watch, then I'll tell you."

I couldn't keep it for three days. We were only into the second when we all gathered in the living room and I told them the story.

We prayed, we laughed, and we cried. Martha has often stated that this final step was the most dramatic and instantaneous healing she had ever seen. The missing pieces of the puzzling struggle had been found.

It was some time before we were able to make any announcements, but finally we told it—to anyone and everyone who would listen: "Dad is finally out of his black hole." "Dad's depression is gone."

*"He brought me up out of the pit
of destruction, out of the miry clay;
And He set my feet upon a rock
making my footsteps firm."*
Psalm 40:2

Chapter 16

Back to Work

Someone pounded loudly on my door. It was just hours following my "deliverance." As I answered, I was given a phone number. Someone had called long distance. I was to return the call as soon as possible.

My good friend, Dr. Norman Lewis, from Portland, Oregon, was on the other end of the line. He explained, "Don, we have a missionary conference scheduled in just a few weeks here at Hinson. In our missionary committee meeting last night it was decided that I should call you and ask you to be our keynote speaker and moderator. Are you free to come and spend an entire week with us?"

"Am I free?" I said. "I've never been freer."

"Would you like to pray about it first?" he asked.

"Norm," I said, "I've been praying for a whole year. Certainly, I'll come. I'd be delighted to be with you."

I didn't know at the time that Hinson was without a pastor. All it meant to me was at least one week's opportunity again to minister.

I arrived in Portland as the guest of Western Conservative Baptist Seminary. The guest room was filled with flowers, large cans of assorted nuts, and a basket of fresh fruit. On the table was a warm greeting from my dear friend, Dr. Earl Radmacher.

Hinson is a church with 100 years of history, filled with tradition and memories. Some of the greatest have served as its pastors. Its honored place among Conservative Baptists had been earned and well deserved.

And it had no pastor.

In recent years the church had been embarrassed by scandal and fractured by division. Its pastors had struggled long and hard to bring about changes they thought would bring it back to life. Its membership had declined, its attendance was down, and so was its morale.

It was peopled, however, by some of the most faithful and loyal Christians I have ever known. They had refused to give in to discouragement. They were convinced that their church had a future as well as a past.

As I walked through that week with them, I enjoyed every moment—recapturing old friendships, sensing God's presence, experiencing His power.

We were praying for an exorbitant Faith Promise goal. We reached it that Sunday. On Sunday evening scores of young people came forward to give their lives to God.

I couldn't have been happier.

During the week, one after another came and asked if I'd stay. Dr. Walter Johnson was the first. With tears in his eyes he said, "Reverend Baker, I think God wants you to be our pastor." Kermit Miller, Frances Peters, and many others said they just felt compelled to ask me if I would be available.

I found it extremely difficult to suppress the wonder and the amazement at what I was hearing and feeling. "Could it be possible . . . ?" "No, not Hinson, not after where I'd been," I thought to myself.

Two members of the pulpit committee visited with me. They both asked numerous questions. We chatted and we prayed.

The deacons asked me if I could stay over and meet with them. I didn't tell them I had nothing else to do; however, most of them knew.

As we met together it became increasingly obvious that God

was doing something—in me—and in them. It seemed that in spite of what they knew they wanted me to be their shepherd.

They asked, "If you become our pastor, what will be your program?" Without a moment's hesitation I said, "I haven't the slightest idea," and I meant it. I had finally learned that churches, like people, are all different, with personalities of their own. It's impossible to superimpose one church's program on another. "But God knows," I continued. "The Holy Spirit will lead us. It may take time, but He will show us."

In that meeting I told them about my depression and about Ward 7E. I wanted no surprises. They deserved to know the worst. I asked them to call the chief psychiatrist and discuss my stay in the hospital and learn for themselves what had happened.

I explained that I was depressive and with that background plus a blood sugar problem I could possibly give way again if I became exhausted or was placed under too great stress.

All of this was discussed openly and freely with the whole church. Dr. M. L. Custis, my friend and champion, fielded numerous questions. An entire congregation listened and reacted to my emotional struggles.

Then they voted to ask me to be their pastor.

I never questioned for one moment that this was the will of the sovereign God. Martha, John, and Kathy had the same exciting assurance.

When Dick Wahlstrom called to give me the news that the church had voted to ask me to be their pastor, my answer was immediate and positive.

I'm well into my ninth year at Hinson now. No ministry has been more fulfilling or more fruitful. In these years we have all watched pastor and people relax, begin to love each other, and enjoy a totally unthreatened relationship.

In nine years nearly 2500 new members have been added—more than 1,000 by baptism. Attendance has tripled, giving has increased five times. World evangelization is a goal of the entire church family, with nearly 100 of our own young people either in foreign service or presently preparing. The church has moved out in the direction of the poor, the helpless, and the needy. We have given birth to two new congregations, each experiencing more than 300 in attendance.

Laughingly, many have said, "God took a dead man, married him to a dead church, and brought about a resurrection of both."

Soberly, I have said many times, "I am so honored to have the privilege of pastoring a church at a time in which God has chosen to bless."

How does one evaluate this entire experience?

I have stopped trying.

I am content today to marvel at a God who loves to take the weak things of this world and use them to display His great strength. He has had no weaker vessel than this one through which to do His work.

What have I learned from this experience?

New insights continue to come into focus daily. I see my God, my self, my family, my Bible, my congregation, and my ministry much more clearly than ever before.

I learned that I am depressive—not always depressed, but depressive, and find it necessary to continually medicate to control my unpredictable mood swings.

I learned that I'm part of a great company of depressive people. The word *depressed* strikes a more responsive chord when I speak it publicly than any other single emotional illness.

One doctor told me that 15 percent of the world's people inherit a tendency toward depression and are helpless when it strikes.

Whenever I speak of my depression, scores of Christian people whisper their thanks and acknowledge their own struggle.

I learned afresh the great value of constant exposure to the Word of God. Lies do not find their origin in God. "God is not a God of confusion" (1 Corinthians 14:33). "In Him [God] there is no darkness at all" (1 John 1:5). The negative thinking that prevails in the black hole of depression can only be countered by the positive Truth of God. In my lucid moments the best defense I could find was to move back into Scripture and allow God to speak.

I learned not to believe everything my feelings tell me.

Feelings need to be understood and sometimes even honored. Feelings, however, are fickle and often determined by physical conditions or external circumstances. I *felt* condemned. I *felt* unloved. I *felt* unwanted. Those feelings were real but they were not valid.

My relationship with God was just as secure and genuine during my darkest hour as it had been on my brightest day.

Romans 8:1 kept coming back to me and whispering over and over again a simple truth that my emotions attempted to reject—"There is therefore now no condemnation for those who are in Christ Jesus."

Even though I was unaware of what was happening, my ten weeks in Ward 7E had been weeks of unconscious ministry.

The Holy Spirit, though not perceived, had been at work.

Men were constantly coming to me for counsel. I had been selected by a group of twelve alcoholics to be their chaplain.

Men were saved in Ward 7E.

The unconscious fragrance of a new-covenant relationship was being wafted through those corridors from the life of a Christian who "felt" that the Holy Spirit had long since deserted him.

I learned not to believe everything Satan tells me.

The deceiver, who is constantly at work accusing the brethren (Revelation 12:10), is always attempting to overload our spiritual circuits with guilt. These constant overloads often result in total power failure.

One way to distinguish whether our feelings of guilt are false accusations from Satan or true convictions from the Holy Spirit is that Satan's accusations are general and nonspecific. They take the form of constant reminders that we are not worthy or that God could never love such as you and me.

In sharp contrast to this, however, is the convicting work of the Holy Spirit. The Spirit of God is specific and always points His finger right at the actual instance of sin. He is not the author of confusion, but very carefully convinces of a specific act that needs to be confessed and forsaken.

When guilt comes and persistent searching fails to determine a just cause for that guilt—write it off as another lie from the father of lies, the devil himself.

I learned not to believe everything man tells me.

When man says, "Depression is a sin," don't believe it. Depression is oftentimes caused by sin, but depression in itself is not a sin. When they say, "Christians don't get depressed," don't believe it.

Moses, Elijah, David, Jeremiah, Jonah, Paul, and even Jesus in His humanness all displayed the symptoms of depression. David even referred to his soul as a "cast soul"—a "soul in despair" as he encountered the pains of depression.

Norman Wright has said that in many cases depression is a healthy response. Depression is a normal reaction to what is happening to a person psychologically and physically. Depression is a scream, a message that some area of life has been neglected. A person should listen to depression, for it's telling him something that he needs to know.[1]

Depression, though its message is often confused, is not telling him, however, that God has deserted him or that God's forgiveness is no longer his.

The screams of depression should never be allowed to drown out the whisperings of God's assurance of His love for us and His presence with us.

What was the cause of my depression?

I do not know.

I've told it like it happened. This story is true.

To attribute it all to Satan gives him more credit than he's due.

To blame it all on the physical discounts all the confused notions and feelings that were a very real part of me.

To blame it on pride, ambition, self-glory, seems reasonable but still incomplete.

It was probably all of these—and possibly even more.

What I do know is that a gracious God took His loving hand and placed it on the psyche of a very self-sufficient child, brought him to his knees, and caused him to be totally dependent on His adequacy for the remainder of his lifetime.

Why have I told you my story?

I have shared a painful part of my past with you in the hope that you who stand beside a person trapped in his own black hole might understand, be patient, loving, and especially careful not to be judgmental or indifferent.

And my desire for you who suffer in this darkest shadow of life is that you will be able to identify with some part of it and find hope. Remember—you will get better.

Chapter 16, Notes

[1]Norman Wright, *An Answer to Depression* (Eugene, Ore.: Harvest House, 1976), p. 18.

PART 2

THE ROAD TO UNDERSTANDING

Emery Nester

Chapter 17

Walking with Don Baker

A phone caller told me about Don's withdrawal. Alone in an Isla Vista beach apartment, he sat with curtains drawn and emotions broken down. Bob Gillikin, my brother-in-law, had called to see if I might get in touch with Don—and help him.

Fifteen years had gone by since Don and I had been together. Similar desires and pursuits had thrust us into each other's worlds. We were both early members of Evangel Baptist Church in Portland. Both attended the same undergraduate university. Both aspired to the pastorate. And both of us did become pastors in the same fellowship of Oregon churches. But in spite of all of those shared experiences that might have provided the tight bonds of a close relationship, the friendship had been casual. Something less than genuine.

And now this casual acquaintance was to be the basis of a counselor-counselee relationship. I questioned the success of such an idea. How could I help Don deeply when our past association had been so shallow?

This was not the only jeopardy we faced. From the very first time I met him and began to know of him, I had felt alienated from Don. Early in our ministries, I saw him and a particular group of ministers in our denomination as snobs who were aloof from me. I did not feel wanted or liked by them.

These negative thoughts about Don didn't arise simply from his responses to me.

My own inadequacies and my early struggles to accept who I was led me to compare with others. I compared myself with Don and his seeming place of prominence. This put further distance between us.

There were many things in my own life I was just now beginning to work through.

I was a dropout from high school. I had a severe speech disorder. I had spent most of my adolescence in the armed forces and experienced an unusual early social life. I had many personal doubts about ever being a successful pastor although this was the desire of my heart.

All of these negative concepts of self became the filter through which I interpreted Don's and my relationship. I did not realize that Don shared similar negative feelings about himself.

When I heard that Don was in Isla Vista in this sad condition, old tapes began to play. My first thought was, "It's finally caught up with him. His problems have gotten the best of him."

But he was a servant of God—laid aside and hurting. I sensed a concern and a responsibility. I had heard this man was being used by God in some unusual ways, so I stepped into the role of helper, determined to get to know him and be involved intimately with him.

After Don and I entered our therapy relationship, my attitude toward him began to change. After approximately 100 hours spent together, his attitude toward himself had changed. He was a different person.

I saw him originally as a trembling, helpless person, desperately wanting to be free from depression. He made some commitments to me and took therapy seriously. He promptly kept every appointment. He discussed inner feelings, distorted thinking, and anything else that might be related to his emotional illness. He opened up to my suggestions. And he worked hard to get well.

As therapy progressed, I saw Don in a new way.

He was human after all. I laughed with him, cried with him,

and felt some of his hurt. I learned something of his heart, the things a person can only learn when walking alongside a wandering, searching soul.

He would talk of contemporary thoughts and struggles. He missed his family. There were fears concerning how he would make a living. There were struggles relating to his church family from which he had been ruthlessly pulled away. Many personal problems from long ago surfaced.

I became a big ear for Don. And he opened up his inner life to me. During that process, we both changed. And I began to know this person I previously labeled "aloof."

As we neared the end of our counseling journey, I felt Don had become a real person.

He exhibited a quality of humanness that was fresh to his personality. Sensitivity to his own and others' feelings had deepened. He now distinguished what it meant to be an effective servant. He understood more about succeeding in his work without falling into the pit of depression again.

A final sign marked the end of his therapy with me. And that was the sign of our true Christian friendship. Here was a man I loved and respected, and one who loved and respected me.

What I wish to say at this point is not easy to talk about. Yet these thoughts complete the story of my feelings about Don.

Don has graciously stated that he owes his ministry in part to me and my help during his darkest hour. And now he significantly ministers to me each week.

Two years ago Don became my pastor. I now experience the way God uses him. Our church is bound together in love and unity. From week to week, people respond to the invitation of the Savior and experience new life. Hearts are warmed and lives stabilized in the context of faithful biblical preaching.

Don has also become a model to all of us in his openness and honesty as a human being.

The ancient Zaddik order of rabbis in Poland became touchable and accepted things naively and at face value. Their humanness enabled them to find an unbelievable acceptance into people's hearts and lives. In much the same way, Don models humanness and down-to-earthness and has found a place in the lives of countless multitudes.

If having some part in this man's continuing ministry had been my only service to the Savior, it would be enough. Based upon this fact, my life could never be in vain.

Section 1

The General Nature of Depression

Chapter 18

Types of Depression

*D*epression has many faces.

It can be the experience of a youth who has learned that he must succeed to please his parents. But he does not live up to his parent's expectations and he feels rejected, unable to please. He gradually withdraws, sinks into a depression, and ceases trying. He sleeps much, eats poorly, and may contemplate taking his life.

Depression can be an unwanted intruder into the life of a middle-aged man. Although well-trained academically, he has no control over his life experiences. He suffers a life-disabling disease that takes the sharp edge from his thinking. He loses his job to a younger man and learns he is unemployable. It is too late to retrain. Life opportunity seems to have completely slipped from his grasp. He has nothing to do, no place to go, and no way to support his wife. These circumstances and losses cause him to slip into a deep trough of despair and hopelessness. There is no way out of the corner.

Depression is a common problem of the aged. The typical retired older person is a widow living at poverty level. During earlier life, she experienced depression from time to time. Now she is alone. Her life seems to be without meaning. Her friends are mostly gone. She is neglected, moved from place to place, and no longer included in family social activities. Such typical experiences of the aged contribute to withdrawal, lack of concern for self, and severe mental disorders which include depression.

As we can see, the types of depression cannot and should not be lumped together under one category. Depression cannot and should not be stereotyped from one individual's experience.

There are several kinds of mood disorders.

One disorder may be characterized as circular with wide swings. Margie will from time to time slip into a deep, prolonged depression with no seeming cause. Her depression continues unending for months. Gradually, however, she feels better and moves to a place of elation and hyperactivity almost as disabling as her deep depression. Over many months and years, she repeats the process again and again.

Another disorder might be like Jeff's experience. He simply feels like a failure with no control or ability to help himself. He sinks into a deep, stable, depressed condition.

Different times of life seem to make some more vulnerable to depression. The later years are particularly rough.

Certain personality types exhibit a proneness to depression. It is much easier for an individual who is perfectionistic with a sensitive conscience to get depressed than it is for a person who possesses a carefree approach to life.

Depressive conditions even appear to occur more often in some families than in others, though usually not in an immediate family. This would be true of such disorders as manic-depressive psychoses that appear to have genetic bases. Usually this disorder can be found in several members of a family tree.

Depression knows no timetable for our lives. It may occur during any period of life. We will discuss the susceptible period of the middle years under the heading *Involutional Melancholia*. But as we have already said, another period of life when many confront depression is old age. During these years, personality characteristics are accentuated; our defenses are often much weaker. A tendency toward depression in earlier life will often lead to serious depression during old age.

One personality type leads all others in its candidacy for depression: the obsessive-compulsive. His overly conscientious character displays itself in an excessive concern with conformity and adherence to standards of conscience. He is markedly inhibited and overly dutiful. This sensitivity of the perfectionist often results in depression when he feels he has fallen short of certain standards. Because the obsessive-compulsive blocks the expression of his anger, he may be more prone to turn it inward on himself and therefore become depressed.

Four types of depression give insight about some general causes for the malady. Understanding the dynamics of each one sketches in a little more of the diagnosis outline with which a counselor works.

REACTIVE DEPRESSION (DEPRESSION CAUSED BY ENVIRONMENT OR CIRCUMSTANCES)

Susan has been married for thirteen years. Although her marriage has not been perfect, she considers it satisfactory. She deeply loves John, her husband.

One day John indicates he wants a divorce. There has been no quarrel or other precipitating event. Efforts to change his mind, to dissuade him from this decision, fail. And John moves out and begins divorce proceedings.

Susan feels deserted. She has not worked outside the home since she married John. She doesn't know what to do. Inwardly she is angry with him for deserting her but dares not show this overtly. She becomes deeply depressed.

Environmental circumstances are by far the most significant and important causes of depression today. Some counselors who have spent their entire lives treating depression have found that every one of their counselee's problems were related to the counselee's environment.

Reactive depression is a reaction to a significant loss. The loss is perceived as unpleasant, harmful, or devastating. Examples include losing a spouse, a job, a reputation, or meaning in life. Coupled with the particular loss is an unrecognized anger. This anger is subsequently turned inward. In this position, the depressed person has made himself the object of his own anger and feels "down." Anxiety naturally follows and joins the feelings of depression.

INVOLUTIONAL MELANCHOLIA
(DEPRESSION OF THE MIDDLE YEARS)

Thelma is a woman in her early fifties. She has been a homemaker for twenty-eight years. Her children have married and have established homes of their own. Thelma tried returning to school but felt unable to compete with younger students. Her marriage has been mediocre, and in many ways she feels trapped by it.

Her husband shows very little interest in her. Affection is gone. Communication is poor. It seems that hopes for life held earlier in her experience are unrealistic. She no longer dreams. Harsh reality pushes her toward the conclusion that there will probably be nothing else in life for her.

In the midst of these circumstances, Thelma sinks into a depression that is much like a stupor. She exhibits little reaction to anything. Mornings are more severe than other times of the day. She is plagued with guilt feelings. She suffers severe weight loss. She would probably be diagnosed as suffering from involutional melancholia.

Involutional melancholia is a depressive disorder that occurs during the middle years of life. The onset does not directly relate to a life experience. Instead it stems from a general feeling of discontent about a person's circumstances in life and a belief that what is left of life is not worthwhile. Such an evaluation is not based on thoughts that are within the depressed's ready reach. These thoughts are either at the periphery of consciousness or are fully repressed. Only severe depression remains in full consciousness.

Men also struggle with the themes of love and relationships into the middle years. But a man's profession and its demands to keep in step threaten and disturb him more. This professional threat can become an obsession, and a man eventually finds himself unable to make decisions. Paralyzed in this state of indecisiveness, he resents having to depend on others. Everything seems to be slipping away. All is about to be lost. The resulting severe depression takes hold when an individual can no longer see a way out. Worry, anxiety, agitation, and sleeplessness are a man's common bedfellows in this condition.

PSYCHOTIC DEPRESSION

Consider a situation in which a teenager makes a meager but realistic attempt to take her life. She is trying to hurt her mother who has been too harsh and strict. The daughter survives, but the mother, who is distraught and feeling guilty, loses contact with reality. She is convinced that her daughter is dead. Her daughter appears to be alive, but this is only a trick of the doctors. She thinks her daughter's eyes are really propped open with tiny toothpicks. This severely depressed woman would be diagnosed as a psychotic depressive.

A psychotic depression is a reaction to a severely disturbing life event. It impairs the ability to test reality and to function in normal ways. In this sense, it is an acute form of depression which may last for a long time.

In a psychotic depression, the individual considers his depression justified and so he desires to maintain it. A drastic change in his appreciation and approach to life occurs.

MANIC-DEPRESSIVE PSYCHOSIS

Arthur is a man in his late thirties. He is a professional with a good position and an adequate income. Twice in his earlier adult life he has been deeply depressed, although there are no identifiable reasons for the disorder.

His latest encounter with depression began after a rather lengthy period of hyperactivity. This period included not being able to sleep well, excessive talking, and an over-elated state. During this time he would go to the home of neighbors at 5:00 A.M. and awaken them. A period of relative normalcy followed the manic period and gradually gave way to a deep depressive condition which continued for many months.

Manic-depressive psychosis lists as a severe type of depression and a major emotional illness in today's society. A sufferer's mood can swing from the depths of depression to the pinnacles of elation. These wide mood swings may disappear from the manic depressive's life only to reappear at a later time. The result is an inconsistent life of normalcy interrupted by unpredictable highs and lows. Remission that seems complete dissolves into a reoccurrence. Because no related environmental event can be seen as the trigger for this type of depression, some consider manic-depressive psychosis to have a genetic or biological basis.

Manic-depressive conditions often respond well to drug therapy.

The chapters that follow share practical insights related to the mood disorders. The next chapter considers depression and its relationship to how we see ourselves.

Chapter 19

Self-Concept and Depression

A counselor on the hospital staff gently probed Don with this question. "How do you feel *about yourself?*"

A description of his own condition formed in Don's mind: "Inadequate! My self-confidence has hit bottom. There is a total loss of self-esteem. . . . I'm a failure."

A visit to the hospital by Don's wife brought more of those thoughts into his consciousness. "I saw myself stripped of all pride, all accomplishments, and all glory. I saw myself as a derelict who had reached bottom. I felt terribly unworthy of this woman I loved so much."

Depression has a way of making a person feel insignificant, unworthy, and of very little value.

In the midst of a battle with depression it is difficult to realistically evaluate ourselves. We see only the negative, the flawed. We have a negative self-concept. Observing this correlation, many attribute depression to negative self-concepts or "negative self-images."

In this chapter we will see what self-concept is and show how it relates to depression.

Let me hold up a caution flag here for our thinking about self-concept and depression. Although negative self-concepts seem to accompany depression, they do not cause depression. Here is a clearer statement: A positive self-concept will fortify us against depression.

Each life experience affects the way we see ourselves, our self-concepts. But if our self-concepts are more positive than negative, the losses we encounter—such as those feelings that bombard us in a depression—will not totally devastate us. We will absorb the negative experiences instead of them absorbing us.

WHAT IS SELF-CONCEPT?

We see ourselves in countless ways. Each of these is a concept of self.

Using myself as an illustration, I see myself as a man, a Christian, a husband, and a father. I am a teacher, a past runner hoping to get into running again, a bicyclist, and an owner of German automobiles. I have pastored churches. I am a psychologist and also somewhat of a maverick.

These are just a few of the concepts of self that make up "me." All of our concepts of self are shaped by our experiences in the world.

Concepts of self differ in importance and clarity. Being a Christian is certainly more central and important to me than being seen as an owner of German automobiles. Being a Christian is the most important relationship in my life. We can see, then, that certain concepts of self rank higher than others—they are more crucial.

In much the same way, some concepts of myself are clearer than others. I see myself as a Christian. I have no doubts in my thinking about this. Christ redeemed me, and I stand in grace. To say, "I am a good Christian," however, differs from my claim to be a Christian. And it is not nearly as clear as the previous statement.

When we organize perceptually all of our concepts of self— all of the ways in which we see ourselves—we have formulated a self-concept. We do this unconsciously.

Picture a line extending from left to right. Each of our concepts of self is attached to this line, the most negative being ranked

furthest left on the line and the most positive the furthest right. A dividing line in the middle separates the negative from the positive. If we have more concepts of self on the left or negative side, our self-concept will be negative. More concepts of self on the positive side means a more positive self-concept.

How Does a Self-Concept Begin?

Self-concept begins shortly after birth. It's difficult to determine how we see ourselves at this point. We can at least say we have vague and hazy concepts of self.

Very early in our lives, people who are significant to us respond to our needs. When we are hungry, our crying brings mother with a bottle. The discomfort felt from needing a diaper change may or may not bring a quick response from a parent.

As little children we need to feel secure—to develop trust that though mother is out of sight, she has not deserted us. We also need to be touched, handled, held. (Without human skin contact, infants will simply wither away, becoming victims of a condition known as marasmus.)

We begin to judge our worth from these early responses. If these needs are neglected or ignored, we develop negative feelings about ourselves and see ourselves as worthless. But the opposite is also true. If significant people respond to and interact with us in positive ways, we will form positive concepts of self and see ourselves as worthwhile.

We organize these concepts of self into our own distinctive self-concept and continue to shape it as we mature.

Two Truths About Self-Concepts

Two characteristics are true for all self-concepts.

First, a person's self-concept is stable. Once it has been organized, it does not easily change. We have an inner need to preserve self-concept—to entrench and fortify the self that is. This is true whether the way we see ourselves is positive or not. And so our stable, positive or negative self-concept colors what we see in every situation. We interpret events according to the quality of this self-concept.

We see this process in the behavior of a husband who feels inadequate. Interpreting his wife's general friendliness as flirtation, he preserves his self-concept of inadequacy by over-interpreting his wife's congeniality. (Many couples have relationship difficulties because one or both have poor self-concepts.)

Likewise, a spouse with a more positive self-concept would interpret his wife's friendliness as charming behavior. She is seen as outgoing, gracious, and one who likes people. His interpretation tends to confirm his own positive self-concept. He has an adequate spouse.

The second characteristic of self-concept may seem to contradict the first. Instead, it compliments it.

Although it is stable, self-concept has a characteristic fluidity about it. This means that no self-concept is forever fixed and unchangeably set in concrete. The constancy of our self-concept in interacting with our environments does not prevent slight movements or changes in how we see ourselves.

CHANGING SELF-CONCEPT

Change. The word sounds harsh, almost like the clamor of metal being hammered, of steel being bent. It is a hard, slow, and difficult process. But many people who come for counseling want to change. They want to change their self-concepts.

Effecting a change in self-concept in a series of counseling sessions is not possible.

Many counselees expect a counselor to tell them a few things that will magically change their self-concepts. Such magic cannot be worked with a few special words or a snap of the fingers. When we examine our own responses to statements we don't actually feel are true about ourselves, the result is *not* instant belief and an attitude change. The result is disbelief in the form of embarrassment or speechlessness.

Some suggest that understanding what the grace of God has accomplished for us will give us positive self-concepts.

This thought is nice, and it is a "spiritual" thought. It does sound theological and logical. The only problem is that it doesn't work that simply. Countless Christians who understand their position in Christ and deeply appreciate the grace of God are yet shy and experience predominately negative feelings about themselves.

Looking at Don Baker's story, we remember that he did experience God's grace in a fresh way. In the silence of his depression, he discovered to his amazement that God loved the inactive. He even loved Don Baker. And he hadn't deserted Don. But this realization alone did not pull him from the grip of his depression.

It is possible that the experience of feeling loved and accepted by the counselor may change how a person sees himself. Indeed, working in a relationship with a loving and acceptant therapist may be the first time a person has ever experienced understanding and genuine caring. This may change him some . . . but ever so slightly.

How, then, can we change our self-concept?

We must have experiences that contrast with how we presently see ourselves. Such experiences take place as we interact with the environment. This is a process. It is not simply a matter of thinking differently.

Suppose we see ourselves as poor academic achievers. We must pass a class, complete a degree, or leap over some other kind of academic hurdle in our lives if we are ever to feel that we can achieve. Or think about parenting. If we are ever to see ourselves as good fathers, we must experience ourselves being good fathers.

What Does Self-Concept Have to Do with Depression

First, we must understand that self-concept becomes the screen through which we interpret what is going on around us.

I have already stated that my own negative self-concept became the screen through which I interpreted my relationship with Don Baker. It colored my view of our friendship and gave me negative feelings.

To illustrate further, let's use personal loss as the event being interpreted. If our self-concepts are generally negative, we will interpret loss in negative ways that relate to our feelings of worthlessness. Loss will only confirm how we already feel about ourselves. If I lose my job and already feel like a loser, the loss only confirms negative feelings about self. The concept of being a loser will deepen and encourage depression.

If, on the other hand, I see myself in more positive ways, I will not interpret a loss or failure in negative ways. The loss will be integrated effectively into my total self-concept, a self-concept that is a rich reservoir filled with positive ways of seeing myself. I can even give a positive interpretation to the loss or failure. In this way a positive self-concept becomes a guardian against certain types of depression.

The Word of God clearly suggests the importance of a positive self-concept. In Matthew 22:39, the writer relates self-love and neighbor love. The ability to do both are connected. Paul states in Romans 12:3 that we should think realistically of ourselves and practice self-acceptance.

We have said that self-concept is the interpreter of events as they relate to us and thus a determinant of how we feel about ourselves. This is important for the depressed person. (It is also important for the non-depressed person!)

In terms of self-concept and depression, a second step is needed to help us out of our dark holes. We need to change our negative self-concepts to positive self-concepts through positive experiences in our world. We must help fill that self-concept reservoir with positive ways of seeing self.

During Don's hospital stay, he ministered to others—he pastored. Even when he didn't feel worthy of being known as a pastor, he entered into significant, supportive experiences with others. And a group of men struggling with alcoholism adopted him as their chaplain. This confirmed Don in some of his abilities once again and in the way he saw himself. We all need, and should seek, these positive kinds of experiences for ourselves.

It is important that parents, teachers, ministers, and others involved in human relationships place value on the importance of a person's self-concept. We should work toward helping people have experiences that will result in positive self-concept.

This is not the simple cure for depression. But feelings of worthlessness and uselessness find their source in negative self-concepts. And these are associated with depression.

Chapter 20

The Feelings That Won't Go Away

"*H*ow do you feel?"

Elusive, indefinable feelings skittered through Don Baker's mind during his depression. Unable to pinpoint any feeling that dominated his outlook, he answered the therapist's question with a volley of emotions that pelted him at different times.

"Sad. Empty. Alone. Hopeless. Afraid. Worthless. Ambivalent. Rejected."

Reading the moving narrative of Don's depression leaves us with our own ragged feelings of guilt, embarrassment, worthlessness, confusion, and hopelessness.

Feelings command universal interest and importance. Yet we neglect their influence in our own lives. We will expand our thinking about feelings using part of Don's story, but we must first understand a few basic concepts about them.

BASIC CONCEPTS ABOUT FEELINGS

1. Feelings—right or wrong?

Richard works the night shift at a canning operation. The economy is down. Demand for canned fish is low. The factory cuts its hours back. And Richard is laid off. He feels an emptiness creeping into his thoughts. And he feels down.

Is that feeling right or wrong?

Feelings are neither right nor wrong. They are simply there. What I do with a feeling makes it right or wrong. This is true of any and all feelings I might have. It is a fundamental concept. There is no sin in feelings.

2. Feelings—irrational and subjective.

Betty and Jim invite their neighbors to dinner. Their neighbors graciously decline, but they do so on the very day Jim loses a major sale at work.

Meanwhile, Betty receives a telephone call from the school. Son Jimmy twisted a few of the conduct rules, and he has subsequently been asked to leave school for the day.

When Jim pulls into the driveway, Betty meets him and they exchange the glum news. Wistfully looking across the lawn, the couple wonders about their neighborhood. They feel the community doesn't like them. An irrational and subjective feeling at best.

Feelings are irrational and subjective. We may or may not know or be able to find the basis for them. They can distort our reality. Indeed, they often do! We must seek to understand the nature of our feeling world.

3. Feelings—vital and necessary.

What would "going home" mean apart from those nostalgic feelings about warm memories in familiar places, gentle thoughts of days gone by, and deepened love that stirs for family and friends? Can you imagine hearing Handel's "Hallelujah Chorus" near the end of *The Messiah* and not feeling the surge of deeply set emotion as the audience rises to its feet in unrehearsed awe? How about the absence of that tender protectiveness, that sweet cherishing of life in a parent's heart when he cradles his helpless infant closely at night? What would life be like without that feeling?

Feelings are vital and necessary in our makeup as human beings. Feelings in our lives can bring quality to existence. With little or no feeling, life would be bland and possibly lack meaning. Without the accompanying provisions of joy and peace, salvation would be considerably less enjoyable and practical in this drab world of pain.

4. Feelings—if they are denied.

Gene saw the rebuff from his father coming. He had made the decision to protect the family interests with a sheltered investment of their shared monies. But the investment had gone sour and the money was lost. In front of the families, Gene's father dressed him up one side and down the other, describing him as an "incompetent fool." Gene listened quietly, not arguing.

Now, months later, he still seethes inside. Though he never expressed his anger or even admitted that his father had made him angry, Gene senses the temperature of his hostile feelings rising daily. But he is not aware of the reason for his anger. Initially he had denied it even existed.

If denial of feelings becomes part of a lifestyle, we leave ourselves vulnerable and exposed to the ravages of emotional illness. Feelings of anxiety and anger, when repressed or denied, will move us toward neurotic illness. Inability to adequately deal with these conditions causes less effective functioning. We become unable to deal realistically with our inner lives and therefore less able to grow in genuine qualities of humanness.

5. Feelings—"You shouldn't feel them."

Sally is a frustrated single woman. Incurably full of life until her thirtieth birthday, she had taken delight in her career and cared little for planning much further in advance than the next weekend. Having or not having a husband did not seem to matter to her.

But the birthday that had taken away Sally's twenties had also brought the future into clearer view. And the last few years had increased her apprehension of what a life alone in an apartment would be like without a companion. Her friends had urged, "As a Christian, you shouldn't feel that way." But she did.

When we respond to another person by saying "you shouldn't feel that way," or "why do you feel that way?", we don't help them grow. (I have found it helpful in therapy to drop these statements from my repertoire of responses.) When addressed with these remarks, people naturally respond defensively.

6. Feelings—Learn to feel them.

People need to be taught to feel things. We need to learn to call our feelings by name—to identify them.

Partial or selective feelings as a style can encourage emotional illness. Only when we allow ourselves to experience honestly the full range of our feelings—and then deal effectively with them—will we move to a place of better mental health. With these practices incorporated into our lifestyle, we will begin to insulate ourselves from the possibility of emotional illness.

HANDLING PROBLEMS AND FEELINGS

Humans often cope by "defending" their egos. Many types of defenses exist.

Denial is one defense. Being unable or unwilling to face possible death during a life-threatening disease is often handled by a denial of the entire condition. We defend ourselves from death and its reality in this way.

Repression is another defense that reduces levels of anxiety. We push unwanted and painful experiences into lower levels of awareness where we can forget them and not feel as much hurt. Severe forms of repression produce amnesia, a form of selective or total forgetfulness.

Or consider projection. With this defense we put blame on a person other than ourselves for something we are surely responsible for. All of these maneuvers protect our egos.

These defensive practices, when not overused, are normal and necessary for our psychological survival. When we become too defensive, however, there is danger of developing a neurotic lifestyle. In this context, neurosis simply implies subjective psychological pain or discomfort beyond what is considered normal for a person's present condition. This pain leads to relatively immature behavior. Such neurotic lifestyles seem to be linked to depression.

A person may survive a lifetime with strong defenses and yet have an underlying neurosis that makes life less productive. On the other hand, a physical condition or combination of physical conditions may cause a person's defense system to be less effective. The psyche, or self, is exposed. Problems and feelings surface. Dealing with the problems underlying an individual's neurosis then becomes crucial.

This is often true with a disorder such as hypoglycemia.

Such an illness will weaken the defense system and make ego defenses less efficient. Those neuroses underlying a person's lifestyle will come to the surface. At this point, a person suddenly comes face to face with most, if not every problem he has ever struggled with.

In Don's illness, hypoglycemia activated his neurosis. It forced him to face many old and new issues in his life. This process of neuroses being forced to the surface through weakened defenses is uniquely true for many who suffer "emotional breakdowns."

Without his struggle with hypoglycemia, Don might not have faced many of the feelings and problem areas of his life that emerged during his depression. Some of these areas were incidental and miniscule. In his feeling life, however, they were giants, magnified all out of proportion.

Active psychological problems loomed on the horizon of Don's experience. Formerly out of sight and undetected, these problems robbed him of an efficient lifestyle even when his defenses were intact. But then they became alive, vivid, and tormenting. Some feelings associated with the new conditions could be trusted; others were gross exaggerations. Don had to experience, examine, and deal with each of them the best he could.

Today Don allows himself to feel. He can laugh and cry. He yet experiences anger. We who sit at his feet do know him to be truly human. We know his physical and emotional frailty. He is a weak human vessel through whom God's strength is made perfect.

Can we dare allow ourselves to feel? Dare we be truly human vessels? The "fruit of the Spirit is love, joy, peace, . . ."—human feelings.

Section 2

Helping and Being Helped

Chapter 21

The Helping Family

*B*arbara stared at the darkened ceiling. As she lay in bed, she thought about her husband, Robert, sleeping beside her. It had been three months since he had admitted to her that he was depressed. He had lost weight and missed several days at work. He didn't even play golf on the weekends anymore.

Robert turned fitfully, mumbling a few unintelligible phrases. Barbara wondered if he would wake up and wander into the living room as he had done so many nights before. No. He still slept. That was good. They had talked seriously about help through counseling a few weeks ago, but he had resisted with the plea for "a little more time to straighten things out myself." She began praying little thought prayers, hoping her anxious feelings would die down. Should she encourage him to see a counselor or wait for him to decide? Was he getting better, or worse? Was she part of the reason for his depression? She didn't know what to think . . . or do.

No one can be seriously depressed without the immediate family being involved. Depression impacts the lives of those who live with the emotionally disturbed person. Close friends and associates may even feel the impact from the discouraged, hopeless outlook of the individual trapped in this state of mind.

Am I to Blame?

When a member of my family gets depressed, I may experience many feelings that will cause me to ask myself a whole new set of questions. I may ask, "How have I caused or contributed to this depression?" Pangs of guilt may condemn me. I see the depressed person and feel I am responsible, in some way, for his suffering.

But we must realize this: Depression is the specific result of an individual's own inner dynamics or his physical condition working in concert with those same inner dynamics to cause the emotional ailment. Viewed this way, it is the depressed person's responsibility.

On the other hand, few become depressed totally apart from their family condition. This does not mean that a family member must bear total responsibility or be seen as a major part of the cause of the suffering. But there are types of lifestyles in a family that can contribute in a general way to depression.

Certain kinds of family events or interaction can bring one to a place of seeming hopelessness.

Losses such as death can steal away hope within a family. Continued berating of a family member, such as a mother's ongoing contempt for her gangly daughter, crushes the spirit about the future. Simple non-acceptance as seen in an avoidance pattern sensed by the aging grandparent withers a person's aspirations about himself. These things may relate to the depression of one or more family members. Even in an occasional depression which has physical causes, the family can be involved in the negative environment with which the depressed person interacts.

As a family or a family member we can have a more positive response to depression than misplaced guilt. We might consider the severe depression of a family member as an occasion to evaluate our family structure and how it impacts each person. Loving families who support their members in healthy ways usually experience emotional health. Acceptance and understanding for each person will reduce the incidence of depression.

But no family is perfect. And when a member of our family

experiences depression, there is really no reason for any member to saddle himself with a burden of guilt. At this point it would be wise for the family to spend time in family therapy with a compassionate counselor.

Don's family opened up to counseling sessions for insight. Martha, his wife, and his children, John and Kathy, all got involved. In the end, they received the reward of knowing that their family was "normal, happy, loving, open, and unusually close." This was an assuring word in a troubled time.

A FAMILY'S IMPATIENCE, A SUFFERER'S MANIPULATION

One feeling common to parents, spouses, and siblings of the depressed is that of impatience. When will it ever end? How long will it take him to pull himself out of this?

We can be terribly impatient because of the pain of the depressed person. We feel so helpless as we see our loved one suffer. Why can't he just cheer up? It is hard for those who are not depressed to understand why someone who is depressed can't simply "turn it off."

We are impatient because of the inconvenience we feel.

Our own life routines are interrupted. The style of living we know has been radically altered because of the attention we must now direct to the sufferer. We find our self-styled encouragements make no difference. It is easy to find ourselves longing for a routine of normalcy again and becoming frustrated, even angry, when the condition seems to never end.

Another aspect of the dynamics of depression important to the family concerns the depressed person himself. The depressed person often manipulates others. He or she may think "if only he becomes aware of how severely depressed I really am, he will reverse the decision that has left me so down. Then I will no longer be depressed."

I have known depressed people who I am convinced are actually getting mileage from their depression. Sometimes a husband will use his depression to keep his wife from following through with divorce plans. He uses depression to gain control over another person—his wife.

Manipulation will sometimes work for a brief time to the advantage of the depressed person. Soon, however, he will find a new, fresh, and startling anger from the person he has manipulated. And the sufferer will end up more depressed than ever.

Family members should be aware of such manipulative tactics and gently, but firmly, resist them. In this way we help by not involving ourselves in a whole new set of unhealthy dynamics.

How Can Families Help?

There are specific ways family members can help the depressed person. We will list some below.

1. As previously stated, be patient. Both with the person and with the speed of his recovery.

There is nothing more difficult than "trying not to be depressed." The person can't just "snap out of it." Recovery from any type of emotional illness is a slow, arduous process, with many "ups and downs." The treatment is not like that for physical illness and often can't be corrected with the passing of just a few weeks.

Depression can linger for months. How well I remember the slow progress of my wife Mary Ann. For awhile she would make gains, and we would be greatly encouraged. Then she would once again sink into a despairing state, and we would both be sure she would never recover. This process went on for more than a year.

It is important for a helping family to understand that there will be many periods of gain with intervening lapses.

If we could only evaluate accurately, we would see that the sufferer has not really slipped to a previous low level. Rather, the "up and down" process is gradually moving him to a higher mood level. He is improving. My suffering family member will ultimately be free from the feelings that now impair him.

2. Be willing to listen when the depressed person wishes to talk. Listening in these circumstances includes the following important characteristics.

First, the individual should not be coerced into talking. He should talk only if he wishes to talk. And he should decide how long he will talk. Otherwise he may not feel accepted or regarded as a person in his own right.

I remember Don's comment about his wife's visits. "Only one could sit beside me for those seemingly endless moments of silence when nothing would come and nothing needed to." She was a good listener.

Second, we must try to really listen. We need to be comfortable in the depressed person's world and try to understand it as best we can. He will share things that may be nonsensical to our understanding of life and the events before us. But they are very real to him. And he needs acceptance in the world where he is struggling.

It is not necessary to become the sufferer's therapist at this point. Advice-giving usually isn't helpful, particularly in the form of quoting Scripture or laying spiritual "trips" on the person. He is already confused and feels guilty. We can be helpful if we convey that we really hear him, and that we are honestly trying to understand him.

Hear him! Walk with him! Share his feeling and world! But always remember that the hurting person must ultimately bear the responsibility of working out his difficulty himself.

3. Continue the family schedule and routine as long as the structure is reasonable and healthy.

Meals should be at normal times. Times for rising and retiring should remain generally as they have been. Keep up family recreation. Include the depressed member—if he is willing—in social events that are part of family activities.

There may be a tendency for the depressed person to want to sleep continuously or withdraw from eating meals or other family activities. Normal family expectations and familiar patterns will encourage the depressed to "stay involved." A stable, normal home atmosphere helps the family as well as the person who is "down."

4. Encourage the depressed to be involved in some new activity. Help him choose things he has always wanted to do but for which he has never had time.

One person I remember had always wanted to take up sailing. He acquired a small sailboat, maintained it, and spent hours sailing in the harbor. Both the time occupied, as well as the contact with nature and the sea, were helpful activities during his depression. Photography would have somewhat the same impact upon a person. It is time-consuming, puts one in touch with nature and beauty, and preserves select portions of the total experience.

Remember these suggestions about a new activity for the depressed.

Aim for an activity that is available, geographically and financially. It should be interesting. It best serves if it is time-consuming. It should be within the capabilities of the individual. Gardening, painting, photography, or an aerobic sport such as running or swimming are often activities that fit the above criteria.

5. I have suggested that family members are not helpful if they try to become therapists. This needs some emphasis and elaboration.

Too many of us want to figure out "why" a person is depressed.

Even if we could accurately determine the cause, what help would this be? Knowing the causes does not guarantee recovery. As a novice, most therapeutic efforts on our part are actually a hindrance to progress and impede recovery for the person we are concerned about.

Let me repeat. Don't try to be the therapist! Be stingy with advice. Offer encouragement by "walking with the person." Listen deeply. Be a big ear!

Learn to listen even with the "pores of your skin." Open your entire self to hear. In doing this we exercise the gift of encouragement and instill hope. We become true paracletes, true helpers alongside of one who suffers.

6. I have assumed that the family of a seriously disturbed person would encourage and assist in finding professional help for their situation. Sometimes this is not the case.

Too many Christians fear a stigma related to seeking out someone who provides psychotherapy. The psychotherapist simply enables another to sort out his feelings and thoughts. We have all experienced uncertainties and even anxieties when we think about "going for counseling." Don shared his embarrassment over this in Part 1. He also shared his present enthusiastic views toward counseling.

My personal observation as a counselor may be important at this point for the reader who needs encouragement to seek help.

I am a professional psychotherapist. I see people in therapy as a very special group when I compare them with the general population. I spend the significant part of every day, week after week, with them. I listen. I try to feel with them. In some ways, I participate in their struggles.

These valued people are not crazy! Indeed, they are a group of those who have sensed a need to grow. They learn to apply spiritual and psychological principles that enable them to grow. They are open enough to seek the help of another in order to be free and productive persons. These attitudes are not always present in the person who is not involved in counseling.

These statements should help to cure the "leper-like status" many associate with counseling. Both the depressed person and his family members need the cure.

Help should be sought as soon as it is apparent that the depressed person is not effectively handling his condition. This is especially true if the condition is obviously worsening. Routine work becomes difficult—he can't pull himself up—life's picture darkens: delay at this point will only lengthen the time of recovery.

GUIDELINES FOR SEEKING A COUNSELOR

A therapist should have adequate training. This usually means academic work to the doctoral level and supervised training in clinical settings.

In addition to professional competence, Christian counselors have an understanding of a believer's unique place in the world as a child of God. Without this understanding, the counselor will have "blind spots" in working with the believer. Problems can be spiritual, as well as psychological, or a combination of both.

A therapist who lacks a biblical understanding of guilt, as opposed to feelings of guilt, would never be able to walk with a person lacking assurance of salvation. Let me explain. Guilt is theological and objective. We never feel it. Feelings of guilt are more psychological and certainly subjective. If we believed we were without God's salvation every time we felt guilty, assurance would be elusive. On the other hand, knowing biblical means of handling feelings of guilt—confession and restoration to fellowship—provides a means that enables us to keep moving and not be overwhelmed by a sense of sinfulness.

Psychology without an adequate theology will be as ineffective as theology without an adequate psychology. Both are needs for a therapist who is to be effective in the life of a Christian.

The counselor needs to be relational and empathic. If one cannot relate effectively to the therapist, little progress occurs. Satisfied clients often pass along the word about the ease of relating to certain therapists, aiding those seeking an effective counselor.

When medical or physical problems exist, one might consider a psychiatrist as the choice of therapists. A psychiatrist is a physician with special training in mental disorders. If a psychiatrist is not involved, the therapist of choice should be willing to work with a physician if a biological base for an emotional disorder seems probable.

7. Sometimes properly prescribed medication is a great help in handling mood disorders.

Don openly acknowledges his use of medication. For many Christians, however, this is a practice fraught with misunderstanding and anxiety.

I am not a physician. As a psychologist, however, I would urge Christians to carefully examine their attitudes relating to biochemical treatment.

For some kinds of depression, medication can make the difference between a person's continuing to function or becoming totally disabled.

In this chapter, we have attempted to give suggestions to those who want to help a close family member suffering with depression. In the next chapter, we will discuss ways a hurting person can help himself.

Chapter 22

Helping Yourself

*R*obert rolled onto his side. He looked at his watch. Two a.m. He had awakened at the same time every morning these past few months.

The next four hours would be agony. Lying awake. Frustration from not being able to sleep. But relief that at least he did not have to face the day . . . yet. And then promptly and harshly at six, the snapping on of the alarm. Feigning sleep, he would pull the covers close while Barbara got out of bed. And another day would have arrived to demand his participation.

That was hours away, though.

At the moment he listened to Barbara's soft inhaling and exhaling. He was glad she was asleep, because she had told him about lying awake late at night, worrying about his depression.

Robert reflected about his condition. He knew that staying in bed when he was down wasn't the answer. Neither was hiding from his friends. He thought there must be something he could actively do to cause the depressing thoughts to lift. His mind told him there was. But what was it?

No set of specific rules helps each person who is depressed or who suffers from some other emotional disorder. The following things often give support through easing the pain and making the condition more bearable. In some cases, these actions are significant helps in the healing process. However, their impact varies not only because of differences in the basis for each illness but also because of differences in the personalities of those experiencing the illness.

We can improve our poor mood levels by:
1. Developing good aerobic exercise program
2. Maintaining a healthy diet
3. Always hoping for improvement
4. Finding meaning in the depression experience
5. Getting in touch with feelings—especially anger

AEROBIC EXERCISE

I remember a man coming for counseling who had been depressed for many months. Combined with his psychotherapy, I encouraged him to get into a daily running program. His condition was severe enough that he was willing to do anything to get better. Within a few months he was running four miles a day and it seemed he literally ran out of his depression.

Getting into a regular exercise program may be one of the most difficult things we ever attempt while we are depressed. Our lack of energy in a depression makes sleeping or inactivity much more desirable and inviting.

For those who are able to persist, however, exercise becomes one of the most effective means of self-help.

Many physiologists feel that aerobic activities—those that stimulate the cardiovascular system and increase our heartbeat to at least 130 beats a minute—activate natural antidepressants that ward off depression within our systems. In time, improved conditioning of our bodies also causes us to feel more positive about ourselves.

Exercise is a friend to the depressed individual.

The exercise should involve kinds of activities that produce aerobic conditions. Jogging, bicycling, and swimming are examples. These exercises are especially helpful for the depressed individual when done daily. Running and biking will also put an individual in the out-of-doors and in natural areas that are not only beautiful but therapeutic.

Though benefits often come early in the program, we experience the full value only in time as exercise becomes more of a lifestyle.

DIET

Eating properly is another means of self-help. A proper diet should include many fresh fruits and vegetables, whole grain cereals, and significant reductions of red meat and sugar.

Many specialists feel there is a relationship between what we eat and our emotional health. The intent of this book does not include examining this relationship. If there are doubts or questions about the effects of diet upon a person's emotional condition, consult a physician or dietician.

AN OPTIMISTIC OUTLOOK

Developing an attitude of hope when depressed is far from easy. But it is very helpful when possible. Feelings of despair and hopelessness dog the depressed person. It's very easy to think about giving up.

Don's early lifeline to which he held tenaciously was "you will get better." This statement from someone in the hospital gave him support and encouragement. When depressed, being optimistic and having hope are very important. This hope is not groundless because most people ultimately get better in spite of the help they do or don't receive.

An early researcher, Eysenk, found that a significant number of those who are mentally ill will make improvement without help from anyone. What a helpful, hopeful thought! This is consistent with my belief that there are regenerative powers in every human organism that move us toward healing and health. It is particularly true for those of us in whom the Spirit of God dwells.

No physician or psychotherapist ever heals a person. We only provide the conditions under which the healing will take place naturally. Some of these conditions involve the counselor sharing himself, practicing acceptance and empathy, and encouraging openness. But he can never heal.

Yet hope develops in the counseling process. For some depressed persons, the hoped-for improvement would never come without outside help. (Eysenk also found that only part of his research population improved without help.)

We learn during counseling to alter our styles of life and thinking to become more effective. As we gain insight about ourselves, we mature and learn to handle pressure better. We break the recurring cycle of depression as this learning takes place. All of these realizations and steps build our hopes.

When we look at the other side of the coin, we realize that hope must undergird the healing process and the counseling experience.

Counseling is a process. We build new resources and learn about ourselves slowly, in small increments. Lack of visible progress can dull our determination and author despairing thoughts unless we broaden perspectives to include our overall improvement. Hope bargains for the time we need while this happens. Having to bring the painful past and present depression into clear focus—a necessary part of healing—makes hope an even more important ingredient. Remember. You will get better.

FINDING MEANING IN DEPRESSION

I remember well a concept Don and I considered during his therapy. A writer we both had read talked about the "pregnant moment . . ."—that moment when an event or events take on meaning. Any experience in a period of time has meaning for us. This is especially true for Christians.

When depressed, anxious, phobic, or in any other state of emotional imbalance, we can seize the opportunity to learn more about self. If we can do this, experiencing an emotional difficulty may be a rare, insightful time to learn what God is doing in us.

Every experience in time can be "pregnant" with meaning, not only for now but in eternity. We can experience our weakness and the need for God, and obtain a clearer understanding of the suffering of others. We can even get more in touch with our strengths as well as our vulnerabilities.

GETTING IN TOUCH WITH FEELINGS— ESPECIALLY ANGER

Trying to get in touch with many of our feelings when depressed is usually not necessary. Feelings are there and can ravage the individual.

One feeling is different, though. In depression, we often turn anger inward. This process is sometimes described by individuals who say "when angry, I stuff it," or "I just swallow my anger."

We experience relief from our inverted anger when we finally feel it—get in touch with it—and learn how to handle it less destructively. Anger felt is no longer anger turned inward and directed against self. And this will cause a decrease in the depression. It is not easy to be depressed and angry at the same time.

Let me illustrate. Rejection by a loved one commonly causes reactive depression. Anger is certainly present in us when this form of depression settles in. There are feelings of worthlessness and scorn that result from turning our anger inward. The idea of "getting in touch with anger" means to simply feel the anger that is really there. Admit it! "I am really angry with her!" There is no need to be hostile or berate the one who spurns us. But we should feel the anger rather than turn it inward.

These suggestions are certainly not depression cure-alls, nor are they substitutes for the avenue of counseling when it is needed. They may, however, significantly aid in the healing process of a depressed or otherwise emotionally ill individual.

Chapter 23

Helping Your Children Be Non-Depressive

A pproximately 50 percent of the people who come to me for counseling related to depression have not reached their thirtieth birthday.

This seems strange. Surely childhood, adolescence, and early adulthood are more carefree times than middle and old age. Yet this is not evident when we look at the age categories for depressed people.

Some describe the generation of young adults at this period in our century as the generation of depressives.

I want to suggest ways parents can move a new generation away from depression as a lifestyle. We can avoid mistakes in child rearing that may prevent depressive qualities from appearing later in our children's adult lives.

LEARNED HELPLESSNESS

Seligman has given us a relatively new approach to the dynamics of depression. He calls it "learned helplessness."

Basically, learned helplessness describes the experience we know as depression. It is a condition an individual finds himself in when he believes that his person and actions do not make a difference. As a result, he gives up, puts forth no more effort, learns to be helpless, and becomes depressed. Only when he experiences his actions making a difference will he no longer be depressed.

My generation may be partly responsible for the depressive characteristics of the present generation. We may have eased the demands of life for them so that they learned to be helpless.

We remember well the struggles of those difficult years of economic chaos—the era of the 1930s when so many of us and our families struggled just to help pay for food and a roof over our heads. As we bore children later, many of us chose to not let our young people struggle as we did. We gave them everything they needed and wanted without their doing anything for it. "Getting without doing" did not teach them that their actions made a difference.

Our parents reared us differently.

We struggled, worked, and accomplished. My parents contributed nothing to my support or education after I reached the age of sixteen. The last money I received from my family after I was seventeen was a $100 wedding gift. I have been responsible for providing funds for my college, seminary, and graduate work. I have paid for every automobile I have owned, every house I have lived in as my own, every suit of clothing I have worn, and every vacation I have ever taken. Though my life was difficult I have seen that my actions have "made a difference." I have invested effort into what I have received.

I had often felt I would have appreciated help. And I helped my children as they grew up. But perhaps we do our children a favor when we don't give them everything. When they struggle and accomplish they learn that there is a true relationship between the effort they put forth and what they get in return. In these ways they learn that their actions do make a difference. We may be effectively helping them avoid a depressive lifestyle characterized by learned helplessness.

ANGER TURNED INWARD

In reactive depression, we sense loss and the consequent

anger about that loss is turned inward and dumped on self. Having made ourselves the object of our anger, we feel down. This is similar to what we feel like when another person is severely angry at us. Except we are now that angry person.

Let's talk about "anger turned inward" as a model we give our children. As Christian parents, we may overvalue tranquility, practice "peace at any price," and feel that anger itself is sin. Many of us would do anything in our power to not be angry or show anger outwardly.

Such behavior either directly or indirectly teaches our children to handle anger by repression (not allowing ourselves to feel anger) or denial ("Who me? I'm not angry!"). We may be helping them to become depressives in this way.

Anger as an emotion is not sin. Learning to experience anger without becoming aggressive is more realistic than repressing it or denying it. As Christian parents, we need to allow ourselves to feel angry and resolve it without sinning. We then become effective models for our children. We need to teach our children to keep anger where they can deal with it satisfactorily—up front, in full consciousness, where they are aware of it.

When dad is angry with mother because dinner is consistently late, he allows himself to be angry and says, "I am really angry that I am unable to keep myself on a realistic evening work schedule because meals do not seem to be on time. It is difficult for me to understand why this must be true night after night. Could you help me with this?"

Or perhaps mother is really angry with dad because he constantly leaves things lying around and the house seems messy and cluttered. Mother allows herself to be angry and says, "I spend much of my time every day trying to keep the house straight and orderly. I get terribly frustrated and angry when I have to go back over the house again and again. Too much of my time is spent this way. Won't you help me?"

In each of these examples, the parent allowed himself to be angry. They described their feelings accurately without personally blaming the other and requested help from the other with their problem. Children will pick up on this kind of modeling.

ADEQUATE, CONSISTENT DISCIPLINE

Realistic, adequate, and consistent discipline plays an important part in our children becoming optimistic, happy adults.

By realistic I mean a disciplinary action that is tied closely to the misbehavior. Adequate means discipline that is appropriate for the misbehavior. By consistent we emphasize that the child should be aware of the gravity of the situation and know what to expect every time the misbehavior takes place.

When we ignore realistic, consistent training of our children, we encourage depressive lifestyles. Remember Seligman? Responding appropriately to our children's misbehavior or inadequate behavior helps them feel their actions do make a difference.

Healthy discipline does not call for excessive, unrestrained force. If we over-discipline, we can put an intolerable burden upon the child.

Look at the discipline of the Lord in contrast to this. Scripture teaches that God's discipline of His children is always in grace. It is never as much as we deserve. His actions toward our behavior have discipline in mind, not punishment. The difference between discipline and punishment is that the former is well thought out, never a reaction, and always has an ultimate purpose that involves our development.

Do we as parents practice these positive characteristics of discipline?

I recently heard of a father who was exasperated because his little son wet the bed. In his anger, the father wrapped the child's head in the wet sheet, upended him, and put him head first into the toilet.

That is not discipline. That is nothing more than undiluted child abuse. It is severe and inappropriate punishment. These kinds of child rearing methods will surely create a depressive lifestyle for the child in later life. The child will end up feeling unloved, unimportant, and dehumanized. Such treatment does not consider the human dignity of a little child.

How can we help a child know that his actions do make a difference?

What are some guidelines for developing principles of excellent, consistent, and reasonable discipline?

Rudolph Dreikur's concepts of logical consequences help us here. As parents, we can set up reasonable consequences of misbehavior and firmly, clearly, and lovingly tell the child what will happen if the misbehavior occurs again. The consequences need to be directly related to the child's misbehavior. When the misbehavior occurs, the consequence is allowed or made to happen—with no exceptions.

Five-year-old Johnny makes it a habit to leave the table after his father offers thanks. He gets up from the table, plays elsewhere, and no amount of persuading will get him to return to the table during the normal course of the meal. Just before the family finishes dinner, however, Johnny returns to the table and slowly eats his food. The family cannot finish the meal in normal fashion. Johnny's actions thoroughly frustrate each family member.

A popular method of dealing with this problem involves threatening to spank the boy. In reality, this reaction reinforces his attention-getting behavior, teaches him how hostile others can be, and perhaps convinces him that a parent can beat up on five-year-olds.

What would reasonable, consistent discipline be in this example? The parent should get down on Johnny's level and look directly into his eyes. Without anger, the parent should say something like "Johnny, we want you to eat dinner with the family. If you don't want to, however, you don't have to. If you choose not to eat with us, you will have to wait until breakfast to eat again. There will be no snack. You make the choice!"

If Johnny doesn't remain at the table, let him go. But he will not eat until morning in spite of his arguing and crying. He will not die of starvation if he waits until morning. In all likelihood, he will be a full-time participant during the next meal.

The principles in this illustration can be applied to every act of misbehavior. Notice. The consequence, not eating until the next meal, is directly related to the misbehavior, leaving the dinner table. The consequence was simply allowed to happen. Johnny couldn't come back to the table.

Johnny certainly had the ability to change his behavior. Expectations were not confusing nor was his behavior change impossible. And he was clearly and firmly informed of the consequences of his actions.

Consistent, reasonable discipline rather than punishment that is reactive and inconsistent will help our children develop non-depressive lifestyles. They will know clearly what is expected of them. And they will learn the results of their actions.

ALLOWING CHILDREN TO BE IMPERFECT

The Fremonts wanted their son Glenn to do well and handle himself successfully in life. Demanding and perfectionistic, they reared Glenn in such a way that he demands much of himself, is very concerned about failure, and even has a higher I.Q. score than most of his peers. Glenn should become a successful and happy adult. Agree?

Some recent research indicates, however, that children like Glenn have the highest incidence of emotional problems in our society.

If we teach our children that failure is always inappropriate, if we communicate that producing as much as is humanly possible without ever failing is always best, or if we leave the feeling that only top performance is acceptable—we build into them a structure for a depressive lifestyle devoid of human and hopeful qualities. Such children will grow up to be "uptight," perfectionistic adults.

We must accept children in their failures and teach them to see these experiences as valuable in their overall development. We must show them that our love is constant and unconditional. We need to help eliminate anxieties they have about their performance in order that they may be free to do their best creatively in directions of their own interests and choosing.

Boys who show interest in automobile mechanics should be encouraged to tinker, explore, and work on old cars. They may become automotive engineers. Girls who are logical and enjoy debate and public speaking should be allowed to engage in activities such as drama and the debate club. They may become attorneys some day.

If a child's interest moves in a certain direction, but the parent requires perfection—no failure—it may be impossible for the child to become familiar enough to continue in the activity and develop a field of interest.

In these ways, we "train up a child in the way he should go, and when he is old he will not depart from it" (Proverbs 22:6). We help build healthy emotional characteristics for the future and promote stability in our children's futures.

Chapter 24

Changing Your Lifestyle

I watched a man come into the office one day, head and shoulders
slung forward and a terrible grimace frozen on his face. He was
the picture of dejection, blind to hope and deaf to encouragement.
He had spoken to me before about his problems with depression
but was not open to suggestions I had given for improving his outlook. He came to talk but not to change.

Convinced that he was the victim of a depressive lifestyle
deeply rooted in his background and personality, this man pessi-
mistically looked at the years ahead of him. Depression for him
was here to stay.

Many who sit in my office for the first time describe themselves as depressives. They sit down, squirm a bit, and finally say,
"I'm a melancholic." We learn early to classify ourselves in
stereotypes. These rigid descriptions help our minds organize information about ourselves.

But must our feet be set in concrete? Are we unchangeable,
bound to serve sentences of gloom and dismay in depressed lives?
Can these lifestyles be altered? Can our conditions improve, and
can we move to a better place?

I give a resounding yes to those questions. Humans are
process-oriented, dynamic beings. It is possible for us to loose our-

selves from the shackles of negative lifestyles . . . and be free.

LIFESTYLES—WHAT ARE THEY?

The concept of "lifestyle" was introduced by a man named Alfred Adler. Lifestyle might be defined as "a person's unique and characteristic pattern of relating to his world and environment." Lifestyle means the ways we respond to and interact with the events that happen daily. It involves the ways we overcome problems we face.

Each of us develops his own unique lifestyle.

Lifestyles have an important bearing on mental illness. In spite of evidence citing genetic determinants for certain kinds of emotional difficulties, no person is destined to be a depressive. Environments, lifestyles, and what we bring to life are all important.

In this chapter, we will discuss aspects of healthy lifestyles.

Although we might feel that our lives have been characterized by gloom, we can reach a place of joy and happiness. We can be optimistic and enthusiastic about meeting each day. We can awaken refreshed. Excitement about the prospect of the day before us can prevail. But for these things to characterize our mood levels, we must often alter the way we respond to and interact with the world about us.

Through the years I've monitored my own lifestyle and those of my clients. I have observed definite characteristics of healthy lifestyles. These characteristics include the following:

1. Firm commitments
2. An adequate philosophy of life
3. A willingness to be human
4. An inner sense of direction
5. The ability to see myself as unique
6. A model of liberty as a Christian

FIRM COMMITMENTS

Of all the issues involved in personal lifestyles, none is more important than the nature of our personal commitments. Healthy, stable persons must have healthy, stable commitments. Commitment is involved in almost every one of our successes as well as in all our successful functioning.

I see at least four aspects in commitment. *Direction* for our lives is the first.

Commitments have direction. Commitments point toward a person, ideas, causes, or something else that exists. And we move toward whatever we're committed to.

The second aspect of commitment is *total abandonment*.

Such abandonment is demonstrated by one who does not allow danger, disillusionment, or distance to turn him back from his goal. He does not give up when the going gets rough or difficult. Commitment implies never letting go, always hanging on, and being persistent to the end.

Another characteristic of commitment is its *reorganizing aspect*.

Commitment pulls inner aspects of our lives tightly together. Commitment keeps us from disintegrating, from falling apart, from collapsing into a directionless pile of rubble.

Finally, commitment calls forth *appropriate behavior* toward its object and direction. It calls forth responsibility, love, and emotion.

Without commitment, we might indeed become depressives. The nature and directions of our commitments determine whether we will become emotionally healthy persons. The authors of this book believe in making Jesus Christ the object of our supreme commitment.

AN ADEQUATE PHILOSOPHY OF LIFE

The characteristic of firm commitments is closely followed by another characteristic common to adequate lifestyles. And that is the characteristic of a healthy philosophy of life.

If life were no more than a grasshopper dance to oblivion, philosophy of life would be no issue. But life is more! Our lives begin, continue, and move us to eternity. We face conflict, pressure, and loss as the norm of our existence. We aren't like the mayfly that is born and dies the same day. Because of the brevity and simplicity of its life, it has no mouth and no need to eat. Our lives are vastly more complex and need a philosophy for living.

What is a philosophy of life? Three aspects of belief or understanding are involved in its definition. We begin to summarize our own philosophy of life by simply answering this question: "What do we believe is real, true, and good?" As we put the flesh on this skeleton question, we put together our own unique philosophies of life.

How can we answer the question "What is real?"

We know of two basic realities—the seen and the unseen. Some of us may accept what we see as our only reality. The reality of the material world. That which enlivens our senses—sights, sounds, smells, tastes, feeling of touch—is the seen reality. This reality includes money, sunshine, other people, the world in which we live.

Some of us also accept unseen reality. Never having seen God who is Spirit, we know there is reality in Him. We believe in a world that is not seen, made up of spiritual, not physical, forces.

We must also answer questions regarding what we believe about truth.

What is truth? What is it like? Where does it come from? How is truth revealed? Is it revealed in nature? What about Scripture and its claims? Are there other written sources of truth, like the Hindu Vedas or Islam's Koran? Can we create truth? Is it relative or absolute, or perhaps both?

The third important consideration in our philosophy of life identifies what we consider important in life.

What do we value? What is good? What is the most important? What are we striving for? For some the answer is material wealth. For others, success in rearing a family is most important. In the life of a Christian, pleasing Jesus Christ is high on the list of priorities. Whatever we value or consider important becomes the answer to "What is good?"

The quality of our philosophies of life determines how effectively we deal with our world. To be concerned only with material things will cause us to neglect that which is unseen and eternal. In a similar manner, allowing my life to be governed by my own truth, and feeling that all truth is relative, will eventually lead me down a path of ultimate destruction and dismay. I simply do not have adequate ability to know right and wrong apart from divine revelation. Nor do I really address things of highest value that do not have Jesus and eternity in view.

An inadequate philosophy of life can map a path for the depressive's lifestyle and other types of mental illness. On the other hand, a sound set of principles, grounded in a personal relationship with God and healthy guides for living, can open the road to emotional soundness.

Try to systematize a philosophy of life. See these principles as governing life today. Ask yourself:

What do I believe is

real, true, good?

You may find your answers totally inadequate and wish to renew, rearrange, or perhaps develop something entirely different for your philosophy of life.

A WILLINGNESS TO BE HUMAN

Christians have often equated humanness with evil. Or with weakness. To be human is to be fallen! If we can deny our humanness, therefore, we deny a part of us that needs rejecting!

Such denial forfeits any appreciation we can have of our development as a person. We shut off characteristics of existence that give meaning to life.

Humanness refers to what is natural for us. It is natural to be hungry, to cry and laugh, to feel things. Humanness spawns feelings of self-preservation. It is human to be weak and to grow old. We are human when we make mistakes. Many of these human characteristics frighten Christians and cause us to try to eliminate them from our lives.

To be healthy, however, we need to see ourselves as truly human and allow ourselves to be just that! Fathers need to see themselves as not always right; mothers as failing their children on occasion; business executives as making wrong decisions; pastors as preaching some sermons poorly, and being too exhausted to do their work as well as they might wish.

Many have observed that as we begin to be the person we truly are, fewer feelings of guilt plague our lives and we experience less depression. When behavior matches feelings, we do not feel so much like failures.

We need to be ourselves without fear! As we begin to live humanly, we set the stage for developing the fourth characteristic of a healthy lifestyle—an inner sense of direction.

An Inner Sense of Direction

People who can make their own decisions, and take responsibility for the same, are people who function most effectively. They are inner-directed.

Being "other-directed" means that we do things because other people believe we should do them. Our lives are governed and managed by the "shoulds" and the "oughts." If this is the chief motivator of our behavior, we set ourselves into a mold or lifestyle that leads to depression.

The apostle Paul is a good biblical example of inner-directed life. In his epistle to the Galatians he recounts confronting Peter for his "two-faced," other-directed approach to fellowship. Peter would not fellowship with Gentiles when Jews were present because of pressure from his believing Jewish friends.

Philip is another example. He followed the inner leadership of the Holy Spirit spontaneously and joined himself to the Ethiopian eunuch in his chariot.

Christians have a unique opportunity to develop inner-directedness. God has chosen to indwell each of us in the person of His Holy Spirit. The Holy Spirit is the true inner Director in each child of God. He is deep in each of our lives. He functions at the seat of our being to control our lives. He is so integrated into our psyches for the purpose of controlling us that we are usually unaware of what He is doing.

As we practice spirituality (living in ways that facilitate the Spirit's control), He guides our movements, our choices, and the directions we take.

"Practicing spirituality" simply means to "walk in the Spirit," be "led by the Spirit," or "be filled with the Spirit." It involves being aware of any sin that has intruded into my life, immediately confessing that sin, and believing that I am again controlled by the Holy Spirit.

In this way, our lives truly become "inner-directed." We do not need people to tell us what we ought to do.

The Ability to See Myself as Unique

Believing and valuing our uniqueness is crucial in the development of a non-depressive lifestyle.

People compare themselves with others. We see someone we admire and realize how far short we fall when comparing ourselves with them. We end up getting depressed! We feel short-changed, ill-equipped, and relegated to second-class citizenship.

The apostle Paul says comparison is not wise.

"For we are not bold to class or compare ourselves with some of those who commend themselves; but when they measure themselves by themselves, and compare themselves with themselves, they are without understanding" (2 Corinthians 10:12).

We also do ourselves a gross disservice when we compare. To desire to be like, to envy the place of, or to compare ourselves with others is to forget the uniqueness granted each of us by our heavenly Father.

We see an example of our individual uniqueness in the face each of us has. Each of our faces has a nose, eyes, a mouth, and two cheeks. There is a forehead and varying amounts of hair on each head. These are certainly similar characteristics. Yet in all the world, except for monozygotic twins, we would be pressed to find two faces just alike.

The same is true for our gifts, our intellects, and our experiences. We are unique individuals.

MODEL LIBERTY AS A CHRISTIAN

The ability to "be free" is a vital part of being one's true self. It is central in the concept of being "inner-directed" and not "other-directed." Let's examine some concepts about "liberty" that free us to live.

1. The only true place of freedom in all the world is that place of being a servant to Jesus Christ. Being a servant and being free appears to be a contradiction. Yet apart from being a servant to Jesus, we are hopelessly bound as slaves to sin.

> "For when you were slaves to sin, you were free in regard to righteousness. But now having been freed from sin and enslaved to God, you derive your benefit, resulting in sanctification, and the outcome, eternal life" (Romans 6:20, 22).

2. As a servant, we are free to regulate our lives and behavior by guiding principles set forth in Scripture. This is particularly true in areas where Scripture gives no direct command.

3. One of the scriptural principles governing behavior alerts us about the responses a weaker brother (one who doesn't understand liberty) can have to our behavior.

> "It is good not to eat meat or to drink wine, or to do anything by which your (particular) brother stumbles" (Romans 14:21).

We should not cause a weaker brother, by our exercise of liberty, to "fall flat on his face" and no longer walk with the Savior.

In the New Testament times, the best USDA grade A beef that could be purchased was found in the idol's temple. A new believer who had previously offered such meat to idols and saw reality in those offerings might be turned away from Christianity by seeing a mature believer eating meat in freedom. He would possibly no longer walk with Jesus.

4. Even though a weak brother has a "conscience" against a behavior, this does not mean that we should become "other-directed" and not practice liberty ourselves. Our love for a weaker

brother may cause us to model liberty and help the brother learn to practice liberty himself.

An almost ridiculous example of how distorted a weaker brother's concept might be is that of a man who once told me he couldn't eat peanut butter and jelly on bread because of a biblical injunction to not "mix seed"—i.e., grain and peanuts.

To never practice liberty because a weak brother has a conscience against a behavior would leave us in an unbiblical position. We would miss the pleasure of peanut butter and jelly, and we would forever be regulating our lives according to noninstructed, wrongly-conditioned consciences. Our behavior under these conditions would continue in a maze of immature thinking with no modeling of the freedom which is truly ours in Christ.

5. Because Christians still fail, we need to talk about feelings of guilt that a condemning conscience stirs up when we do fail.

Many years ago in Los Angeles, I heard a radio minister say, "Conscience is a heavy footprint of God upon a man's heart." That is not necessarily true. In man's original condition, conscience may have been a perfect indicator of right and wrong. Today, however, conscience is more often the "heavy footprint" of man's social conditioning.

We can be conditioned to feel guilty about any type of behavior, even if it isn't sin. A weak brother has been conditioned to feel it's wrong to eat peanut butter and jelly on bread. Certainly this is not sin. Conscience may or may not be consistent with the will and holiness of God.

Guilt is objective. We never feel guilt. It is a condition that exists when I violate the will or holiness of God. "Feelings of guilt" are subjective. It is "feelings of guilt" that hurt. They may or may not be actually related to true guilt.

When I bear false witness, I am guilty. I may or may not experience guilt depending upon my understanding of this behavior as sin and my own sensitivity. This depends upon the nature of my early conditioning and my knowledge of Scripture. The better my understanding of the Word of God, the more appropriate my feelings of guilt will be.

There is a movement in Christian psychology to eliminate

confession as a practice, even when we are aware that we have sinned. Yet confession plays a vital part in behavior related to forgiveness, restoration, and freedom from "feelings of guilt" (which are related to guilt when we have sinned). Only as we learn to confess sin in our lives can we experience the removal of guilt and have freedom from an oppressive, guilty conscience.

This chapter ends with the hope that, using some of the characteristics of healthy lifestyles, we can evaluate, alter, and enter a lifestyle that will be depression-free.

Section 3

The Unmentionables

Chapter 25

Suicide

*E*arly in my pastoral ministry, I shared the anguish of a young husband whose wife took her own life. Having just given birth and apparently suffering from a postpartum depression, this young woman left her home during the night. She was found later face down in a flooded field behind her house. She had drowned herself in about five inches of water from the spring overflow of the small river nearby. The young husband grieved deeply over the loss of his precious wife.

Suicide is a problem among Christians as well as among society in general. Some who read these chapters have lost a loved one or friend in this way. Others will experience suicide, or the threat of suicide, in their families at some future date. Some may even be contemplating suicide as they read this sentence.

The Relationship of Depression to Suicide

It is unlikely that suicide will occur in isolation from depression. I have never known an individual who enjoyed an optimistic lifestyle, experienced success, and anticipated the future with happy expectations to terminate his own life.

Suicide is associated with feelings of despair.

The potential suicide victim feels hopeless. As the deeply depressed person assesses his life situation, it is as if there is no way out of the corner. Life is too painful. There seems to be no alternative left for a person but to take his life.

It is not easy to understand fully what happens when suicide, as an alternative action, at last becomes a real and viable choice. The individual has probably been deeply depressed for some time. Suicide has remained in the person's thoughts as a difficult idea to dislodge. Leaving life looks like the only escape route from difficulties. The pain would then be over. Suffering would cease. As the depression begins to ease a bit, and a person gains a little of his strength back, he makes the choice to put his chosen method into action. And he kills himself.

Suicide happens in the context of a depression that lingers and becomes difficult to overcome. It seldom, if ever, is isolated from the gloom of a mood disorder.

COMING TO GRIPS WITH THE ISSUES

Believers face certain issues with respect to suicide. These questions are not always clear, nor are there ever easy answers. The following are just a few of the issues the Christian world struggles with as the rate of suicide in our subculture increases.

1. How can one who is a leader among Christians, one who is set apart by God for ministry, ever consider such a heinous sin? (Both Don and I have had thoughts about suicide!)

2. Can a person who is sane take his own life?

3. Would a true Christian ever contemplate suicide seriously and take his own life?

4. If one is a believer, does he terminate his relationship with God by this act of self-murder, ushering himself from God's presence eternally before being able to ask forgiveness for his sin?

How could Christian leaders have suicide thoughts? How can it be that some actually end up taking their own lives?

We need to remind ourselves that our pastors, teachers, and counselors are clothed in human flesh like other people. In many respects, these individuals are more vulnerable to stress, loss, family difficulties, and even attacks by the enemy, Satan.

For these reasons, the option of suicide can be just as real for the Christian leader as it is for the lay person. The church needs to pray for and support these choice servants of God.

Let's consider the matter of Satan's direct involvement in suicide. Surely every attack of depression is not demonic. We have talked about biochemical irregularities, environmental factors, and internal personal dynamics as sufficient cause for a person to be depressed. Even suicide can be free from Satan's direct influence.

On the other hand, special demonic activity can bring about the possibility of losses, hindered or hampered relationships, or other situations which could cause depression. Satan's involvement as the "god of this age" can also create pressures at a time of deep depression which may encourage one to end his life.

The suicide of any child of God—a member of His body, the church—is always a sad loss. This is true not only for the immediate family but also for the church itself. Every believer stands equipped with spiritual gifts that enable him to function within a given body of believers. One may be depressed because of feelings of uselessness associated with not developing these gifts. The suicide of a Christian, however, permanently cripples the functioning of the church on earth because of the loss of the ultimate development and use of those gifts.

Consider next the sanity of the suicide victim.

Are not all who take their lives obviously insane? To believe this would, of course, shelter one from dealing with issues like the eternal destiny of the suicide victim. A plea of insanity for a suicide victim would basically absolve him of responsibility for the act.

How do we define insanity? Insanity usually means that a person is not responsible in any way for his actions. An insane person who commits suicide is beyond the ability to make a choice to live. But is this true about the depressed person who takes his life? Can he no longer choose life?

Some who take their lives are obviously insane. Most professionals would agree with this. It is also apparent that many who take their lives do make rational choices up until the point of self-destruction, and they see suicide as the only alternative for escape from their seemingly hopeless situation.

But many suicidal people see and choose additional alternatives to ending their lives. So we cannot attribute suicide to insanity alone. If this were true, no person who killed himself would ever fully understand the implications of this desperately final act. And yet some do.

Does suicide ever become a reality for a true believer in Jesus Christ? The answer is "of course."

The Christian community is no more immune from this experience than from any other effect of sin in the human race.

When the assaults of depression buffet one, suicidal thoughts are common. In a severe, prolonged depression, in the midst of seemingly hopeless circumstances, many believers have taken their lives. These people wrongly assessed their circumstances. They had not explored all of the alternatives. The depression had distorted their thinking. But they are yet children of God who became ultimate victims of a mental disorder which caused them to consider self-destruction . . . and follow through with it.

And then there is the matter of the suicide victim's eternal destiny. Many feel that suicide is the ultimate sin for which there is no forgiveness. Isn't a person who ends life left in a position of not being able to repent or seek restitution?

This is obviously a misunderstanding of the gospel of God's grace. The only sin that truly keeps one from God's presence is the sin of unbelief—of not trusting the work of Christ personally. The inability to confess suicide as a sin is not a real issue.

God's forgiveness gives me a position as His child and deals with all of my sin—past, present, and future. If salvation depended upon confessing every sin committed as a believer, no one would qualify! We have all sinned in ways we either were not aware of or were not concerned about enough to confess individually.

> "Payment God does not twice demand
> First at my bleeding Surety's hand
> And then again at mine."

The unfortunate and sad ending of an individual's life by his own hand does not nullify the effect of the grace of God in his life. Suicide victims who are children of God are redeemed souls in the presence of their Heavenly Father.

UNDERSTANDING AND ASSESSING RISK IN THE POTENTIAL SUICIDE VICTIM

Before leaving this chapter, I would like to make some observations about suicide's occurrence and the suicide victim.

Most people who take their lives have talked about it to someone. This is a way in which they ask for help. It is important to listen and always view any talk about suicide as important. Serious thinking about suicide formulates some detailed plan in the person's mind for carrying it out. We can inquire about this at some point in our conversation with him.

Even though a person has been a suicide risk at one point in his life, this will not always be true of him. Individuals who have been suicidal can again be enthusiastic about the future. "Once a suicide risk, always a suicide risk" is simply not true.

A person who becomes suicidal really has mixed feelings about death. Most would prefer to work out their problems and live. Because of this, most suicidal people do respond to counseling and other efforts that instill hope. No depressed person who appears on the verge of suicide should be given up as hopeless.

Suicide does not "run in families." It is true that family members can pick it up as a model for the way out of a problem, but there are no specific genetic determinants of suicide. Discount this theory!

Most suicides occur relatively soon after improvement begins. The deeply depressed person rarely has enough strength to take his own life. When the heavy cloud begins to lift, however, the time of greatest risk begins. Those who want to help need to be especially alert to the danger at this time.

In concluding this chapter, there are some special indicators of the high risk of suicide that are worth knowing.

The risk of suicide is always higher when there has been a history of previous attempts. These attempts—even if they lack serious intent—weaken life-preserving responses.

There is higher risk when there are chronic self-destruction patterns in a person's life which include fantasy and preoccupation with suicide. This observation is associated with the previous statement.

I remember a college student majoring in art who was obsessed with suicide. In almost every artistic production of human figures, she would include a splint on a leg or an arm indicating a severe injury to the body of the person in the picture she drew. She herself was at that time constantly dealing with suicide as an alternative in her own life.

If a depressed person has recently suffered a severe loss, or is on the verge of a severe loss, this makes risk higher. The loss of a job for a man in his late fifties can be a severe blow in an economy such as that of the early 1980s. With no hope of ever again being employed and with retirement benefits gone, the individual feels there is little to live for.

Sometimes there are those who are unable or unwilling to accept help. These individuals are always to be considered higher potential suicide risks than those who are willing to work on their problems.

Finally, those people with personal inner resoures will be lower risks. Such resources include the ability to relate effectively with others. A person who relates to others does not feel so alone and will find friends to help share his heavy load.

Perhaps the most significant and meaningful resource is a tie to the church and relationship with Jesus Christ as a friend.

Consider these next statements, friends of sufferers and sufferers who are searching. Christ has promised to make every loss a means of personal growth. His friendship is never-ending and closer than that of any brother. He can open alternatives in one's life in most unpredictable ways. And He provides more grace for every trial.

When there is a relationship with Him, there are infinite inner resources. Suicide risk does not have to be as great.

Chapter 26

Hang-Ups of Christians

"*T*he mentally ill are demon-possessed and should be avoided."

"Those who are spiritual do not become mentally ill."

"I would be embarrassed if others learned I have been in counseling."

"It's a sin to be depressed."

"If I truly appropriated the adequacy of Christ, I would not be experiencing emotional difficulties."

"Increased Bible reading and prayer will cure my emotional illness."

"God could never use the experience of depression to conform me to the image of His Son."

Until recent years, the area of mental and emotional illness has been misunderstood and feared by the Christian community. Because of this fear, we feel a stigma if we face mental difficulties in ourselves or in our loved ones. We have developed attitudes that are unrealistic and naive as illustrated in the above statements.

Don talked about some of these attitudes in his narrative. How could a pastor experience what he was going through? Professional counseling really is of little value for the Christian. It is a shameful thing to experience such emotional struggles.

Christians need to be free from this kind of bondage. We need to be free enough to acknowledge our psychological problems and seek appropriate help. As a rule, however, we are too uninformed, too embarrassed, or too fearful to get this help.

In this chapter, we will discuss some of those more common hang-ups that create poor attitudes and prolong emotional difficulties in our lives.

MENTAL ILLNESS AND DEMONIC INVOLVEMENT

People have misunderstood mental illness since the beginning of time. Historically, those suffering in this way have been considered incurable and isolated permanently from society. Care at best was only custodial and in many cases was no better than would be afforded animals. Many were confined in prisons and not a few burned at the stake because of supposed demonic involvement.

During the past 100 years, however, scientific efforts to understand and treat these disorders have greatly increased. These efforts have not gone unrewarded. The public in general more readily understands and accepts the mentally ill. The general populace recognizes psychiatry and psychology as valid healing disciplines.

The overall picture has been somewhat different among Christians, however. We continue to cling to our superstitious fears and distorted thinking in these areas.

Mental illness and demonic activity have been seen by many Christians as synonymous. It would be foolish to deny that mentally distorted thinking and behavior never indicates demonic influence. On rare occasions, Satan himself may attack an individual. He is our enemy. He wishes to disrupt, confuse, and destroy our lives of effectiveness. But when or where there is direct involvement of the enemy would be difficult to judge.

When we attribute the whole scene of mental illness to Satan, we remove personal responsibility for our choices and our behaviors. Satan gets the credit and we get an excuse. The "devil-made-me-do-it" attitude ultimately avoids the real reasons for our condition.

Many of the complex types of mental illness defy human understanding. And so we can easily attribute disorders such as obsessive thinking, compulsive behavior, severe depression, and paranoid delusions to the realm of darkness.

Dean is a high school teacher who hears voices when he lectures. They seem to argue over who will control him as he teaches his classes. They never cease their arguing and Dean is about to go mad. It is easy to label such a condition as demonic rather than the mental disorder of paranoid delusions.

Yet enough imperfection and disorder exists in our world system to create the conditions for a mental problem such as this apart from Satan's direct attacks. We are imperfect creatures. We live in imperfect environments. The "god of this age" could let us alone entirely, and we would yet become mentally ill.

We must face the reality of our imperfect psyches.

We should look at imperfection the way we view physical imperfection. At every period in life, we can develop kidney defects or heart difficulties. This is quite clearly understood by most of us.

Our mental conditions are imperfect as well. Each of us is at least a little bit "neurotic." All of us are capable of developing serious disorders. Understanding this would enable the Christian community to deal more effectively with emotional problems. Certainly we could deal with these problems more effectively when we see their source to be environmental and interpersonal conditions as opposed to demonic or "other-worldly" causes.

"Spiritual Christians Do Not Break Down"

One event forever dashed to bits this fallacious idea for me. And that was Mary Ann's depression. Mary Ann, my wife, has lived a life of sensitivity, serenity, and spirituality. Yet she suffered an emotional and mental breakdown from which it took five years to recover completely.

If we assert that the spiritual do not become depressed, we heap unbelievable feelings of guilt upon the Christian with a mental disorder. Either he must deny his emotional condition completely or bear the heavy burden of failure in his Christian life. Both of these alternatives are unreasonable. They block healing. The disorder only deepens.

We continue to walk imperfectly in a fallen world. Our perfection awaits our resurrection. Only absolutely perfect spirituality—with never a lapse—could ever make us immune to emotional illness.

In reality, we all fail. We all take control of our lives from time to time. We all sin. Those whose lives are characterized by spirituality do fail. The spiritual do react with aggression. They can rationalize away the truth and lie. The spiritual can become faithless. And the spiritual can experience emotional breakdowns. We can become severely depressed.

In some ways, those who are spiritual may have a sensitivity in their spirits that makes them more vulnerable to depression than the average person. They do not have a "seared conscience" (1 Timothy 4:2). The spiritual are sensitive to sin.

PERSONAL EMBARRASSMENT

Jerry was a deacon in a church and a respected leader in his congregation. Unknown to most people, he had a serious problem in his marriage. In order to preserve his anonymity, he urged the counselor to meet him in a bar in a neighboring community where he would be unknown.

One of the most difficult hang-ups Christians face is coming out in the open and admitting there is a problem. We seek professional help with great difficulty.

Christians reveal their timidity about getting help in many ways. Some call for information without giving their names. Others make appointments using names other than their own. The story above shows how some want to meet in neutral places such as a bar, their home, my home, or in the park. Some are even unwilling to use insurance coverage for fear of "being discovered."

Such embarrassment immediately points out how we view an emotional struggle—it is an unreal plague for the weak. We have talked about the need to see emotional illness in the same way that we see physical illness. Then we can see treatment in similar ways. Few are embarrassed to be physically ill. There is no reason to feel differently about mental illness.

Feelings of embarrassment would also diminish if we would see counseling as a "gift of the Spirit" specifically given for needs in the local church. Paul included exhortations as one of the gifts of the Spirit in the book of Romans (12:8). The word "exhort" is from the Greek word *paraclete*—one called alongside to help, one who walks with another. A counselor who is a Christian exercises a spiritual gift when he walks with another member of the family of God.

The church does not fear the benefits of the gifts of pastor-teacher, administrator, or helps. Why should we fear one coming into our lives to encourage us when we experience emotional problems?

"IT'S A SIN TO BE DEPRESSED"

Being depressed is often equated with faithlessness or unbelief.

Let's return to Don's emphatic statement: "It's not a sin to be depressed!" Depression does lower our mood level. It seriously hampers the effectiveness of an individual. It often includes deep feelings of hopelessness and despair. Family and friends will be affected by the pessimism. But these conditions do not indicate a lack of faith. This condition does not place a Christian in an inferior position as a child of God.

It is certainly possible that one can become depressed because of continual failure and sin in his life. Scripture teaches that the one who covers sin will not prosper (Proverbs 28:13). This might be a part of the believer's depression. But depression in this sense is simply a result of sin and not a sin in itself.

A quick summary of depression's dynamics might help here. As a general rule, depression results from loss. We handle loss ineffectively when we have negative self-concepts, less maturity, less autonomy, and thereby do not know how to handle anger. As we experience loss, anger related to that loss is turned inward. We become the object of our own anger. When this takes place, we feel worthless and "down." There may be feelings of hopelessness.

But this chain of events does not mean we have lacked faith or have sinned. Nor does it mean that we have forgotten the promises of God.

"IF I TRULY APPROPRIATED THE ADEQUACY OF CHRIST . . ."

This hang-up is a sister to the idea that if we were only sufficiently spiritual, we would never be depressed.

The adequacy of Christ is ever present as a resource for us in times of difficulty. However, we all appropriate this power in relative ways. We do look to God for support in our struggles. We do remember He has given us eternal life and we are strangers awaiting ultimate transformation. His Spirit does dwell within us and produce spiritual graces. But we do not perfectly appropriate these things.

One might argue in the same way for the end of physical illness. Yet the position that physical illness results from a lack of experiencing Christ's adequacy is unbiblical.

Deliverance from mental and physical illness will ultimately be a part of the healing that Jesus brings through His death and resurrection. Fully experiencing the benefits of this atonement, however, awaits our own resurrection. To argue otherwise only adds to the anguish of a child of God who is in the clutches of a depression or some other mental disorder.

"INCREASED BIBLE READING AND PRAYER WILL CURE ME"

Some believe that increased Bible study and prayer blaze the only path back to emotional health. This is a very common idea among believers who are experiencing emotional difficulties.

This strongly held belief arises out of the zeal with which we instruct people to engage in these practices for their own growth and maturity. And these practices *are* essential if one is to make continual progress in his Christian life.

Mood disorders and other types of emotional illnesses create unique problems of subjectivity, problems that can affect our view of spiritual disciplines like Bible study. A person may feel guilt that is all out of proportion to the behavior which is troubling him. There may be grossly self-centered feelings and thoughts. There may be feelings of deep inadequacy in performance. In this frame of mind, emphasis upon increased Bible study and prayer can actually hinder recovery. One will often move randomly through Scripture and settle in the Psalms where David shares the anguish from one of his own depressive experiences. A depressed person ends up overwhelmed as he experiences firsthand another's depression.

The following are suggested guidelines for Bible study and prayer when the individual is depressed.

1. Try to understand that experiencing depression or another emotional illness usually has little to do with the practice of prayer and Bible study.

2. Though prayer and Bible study are to be encouraged in our daily walk, we should not use them as if they would alleviate the emotional illness we are experiencing. Doing more of these things is not the way out of an emotional wilderness.

3. Continuing planned and well-structured Bible study is good if it does not leave one more depressed and if interest continues naturally. Legalistic Bible study and prayer can impede recovery.

4. We should feel free to discontinue dutiful prayer and Bible study if interest wanes or if one becomes more depressed as a result of such practices. As a child of God, the believer will hunger and thirst both for the Scriptures and for fellowship. In time he will naturally move back to these necessary practices of the Christian life.

EMOTIONAL PROBLEMS AND THE WILL OF GOD

We find depression difficult to integrate into the will of God. Yet Scripture assures us that God deliberately patterns the events in our lives. Each happening becomes purposeful and good. As the pattern unfolds, God moves us toward the ultimate goal of conformity to the image of Jesus Christ.

We incorporate tragedy, loss, physical illness, and other experiences into the will of God for our lives. A large body of believers see emotional illness as different, however. When deeply depressed, we find it difficult to pause and consider how the Father is fitting this experience into His plan for us. It is hard to see what significant learning or new path in life He is opening. In emotional distress, few of us have any thought of creating meaning from the experience or seeking its positive aspects. We just want freedom—from the pain and from the stigma.

We have read Don Baker's account of deep depression. We have probably sensed that, however painful the experience was, there is in the heart of this man a gratefulness to God for what he has experienced. Because of depression, he has become more open. He is now extremely sensitive. He is able to love his people.

Don has learned through his agonizing experience that man's sufficiency is totally inadequate for the position of a servant. In his struggle and confusion, Don discovered that adequacy is found only in partnership with the Father. And Don never meets a depressed person in his pastoral counseling with whom he cannot identify, as he himself has known the lonely pain of that black hole.

The Don Baker of Hinson Memorial Baptist Church today is not the Don Baker of Hinson Memorial Baptist Church twenty-five years ago. The four years of depression and despair are part of God's conforming him to Christ's image. Through this experience, He has equipped him for an unusual ministry. Don will never be the person he was before his agonizing experience. Nor will any of us, if we can see our experiences as part of the will of God for our lives.

Chapter 27

Do Counselors
Get Depressed?

A nd now my own story of depression.
Yes. I, too, have been depressed. As some of my depression experience ironically overlapped with the period of time that I walked with Don Baker, I will complete our story with my own narrative.

I accepted my first position as a psychologist on the faculty of Westmont College in 1967. Certain events during the summer and fall of '69 left me deeply depressed. Common to these feelings was the thought that I was being used like an object by people I valued.

Of course, I had routinely experienced times of minor depression before. Common experiences for a pastor, these "down times" had always been relatively short in duration.

But not this depression. This time it would not go away! I felt dehumanized. All the feelings of being normal emotionally left me. Self-feelings ruled, and I was really down.

My sleep was disturbed each morning at 1:30 or 2:00 and I would toss fitfully until I had to get up for work. Concentration was difficult, and although I managed my teaching and counseling load, my normal lifestyle was altered—cut back—impaired.

As summer faded, I felt myself slipping more deeply into this depressed condition. No amount of effort to "get up" worked for me.

On the day before Christmas I felt like everything was lost.

My sinking feeling accelerated and I could not control the stepped-up emotional pull downward. I was caught in a giant whirlpool of despair. Swirling round, descending, I was utterly powerless to control what was happening to me.

For the first time—ever—I felt that life was not worth living.

I tried to convince myself of the absurdity of that feeling because rationally I knew it was not true. Earlier in the year I had finished my doctorate and experienced an all-time high. But my efforts to convince myself failed. Life seemed empty and meaningless.

On that day, I faced a startling fact—I needed professional help.

Christmas Eve is not the best time to call a therapist. But I called every psychiatrist listed in the yellow pages. (Except the ones I knew.)

Each doctor instructed me to simply check into the county hospital. After all, it was Christmas Eve, and everyone wanted to be with their families.

When I finally realized that no one would see me on an emergency basis, I became very angry with psychiatry as a helping profession. "Where is their commitment?" I asked myself. "What do they really feel about persons in need?" Had I not made an earlier commitment to be available to anyone who really needed me, regardless of the hour or day?

Two significant things happened that evening.

First, I was deeply angered toward psychiatry and the individuals I called. Those feelings of anger somehow lessened my feelings of depression. As I have said, "felt" anger and depression have a difficult time coexisting.

Second, I made a decision that night. I decided to use my depression for learning more about it . . . and myself. I would overcome depression using resources within myself. This depression had to be in the plan of God for me as a learning experience. I decided to try to learn how to make that a reality.

I began reading and rereading everything on depression in my library. I became intrigued with my personal dynamics, my anger, my self-centeredness, and my manipulative efforts that were deeply imbedded in the depression.

I reached a place where it mattered as much to learn as it mattered to not be depressed.

Then one Saturday evening in April I received a call from Arthur Lynip, dean of the college. Dr. Lynip said, "Emery, I'm teaching a class of forty depressed adults at Grace Church. Could you come and speak to them on the subject of depression?"

My response was immediate. "Could I? . . . There is nothing I could do more easily."

In half an hour I had organized my thoughts about what I had experienced during the preceding seven or eight months. The next morning I shared myself and my depression with these people.

While I talked, I felt the cloud of despair lifting. As a cork pops to the top of the water, I felt myself springing out of the gloom that had engulfed me.

When I finished speaking, I was free. I was no longer "down." The hurt was gone. Finding meaning for myself in this difficult experience helped to release me.

Today it's difficult to think that I could have been so depressed.

I began walking with Don during the last five months of my depression. Because our depressions coincided, I could understand his experience and feeling more fully. And my walk with him gave me the meaning I sorely needed at that time.

Now we have written of these experiences with the desire that you who suffer in depression or walk with a sufferer might find hope and be helped. In the plan of God, it could not have been otherwise.

Subject Index

Reactive depression, 123. *See also* Depression, types of
Reality
distorted by depression, 33-35
and philosophy of life, 168
Rejection, 42-44
Repression, 138
Routine, 147

Saloum, Richard, 84-85
Satan
and depression, 98-101
and mental illness, 184-85
and suicide, 179
works of, 97-98, 109
Satanist, encounter with, 98-101
Self-concept, 127-33
change in, 130-31
characteristics of, 129-30
and depression, 131-33
meaning of, 128-29
Self-esteem, 18, 85
Seligman, 157, 160
Sex, 19
Sin, 109-110
Sleep, 18
Spirituality, 185-86
Stedman, Ray, 57
Success, 56-57
Suicide, 177-82
and Christians, 178-81
and depression, 47, 177-78
genetic determinants, 181
potential, indicators of, 50, 181-82
prevention, 47-51
purpose of, 49-50
and sanity, 179-80
and Satan, 179
thoughts of, 19
typical, 47

Therapist. *See* Counselor
Truth, 168

Unemployment. *See* Depression, job loss
Uniqueness, 171
Unworthiness, 24

Value, 168
Vietnam veteran, 60

Weaker brother, 172-73
Weight, 84-85
Will of God, 189-90
Witchdoctor. *See* Olipha
Withdrawal, 41-45
Work ethic, 55-56